The 500 Hidden Secrets of

TOKYO

INTRODUCTION

Japan is supposed to be a monolingual and monocultural country.
Take a closer look at it on a map however, and you will discover that
it actually consists of a group of several islands. The country has many
different cultural characteristics, depending on the regions. There are
hundreds of accents which might be too different from one another
to be considered dialects.

Tokyo, the country's capital, is a microcosm of Japan, attracting people
from all over the country. What do you see in your mind when you think
of Tokyo? A city in manga and anime? A city filled with high-tech gadgets?
A city where people bow frequently even when they are on the phone?
The truth is that, as a city, Tokyo is a bit of a mishmash with many
different combinations. A tall futuristic building is built alongside an old
house. A boy wearing clothes from the latest collection of a French brand
walks hand-in-hand with a girl in a traditional kimono.

You might also think of Tokyo as one of the most crowded cities in the
world. Don't let that scare you: it's true. Tokyo is very densely populated,
but there is so much more to it. It has a great many aspects that are
changing at a rapid pace; hopefully *The 500 Hidden Secrets of Tokyo* will help
you discover new sides to this city that you were unaware of, and will
inspire you as you organise your holiday here.

HOW TO USE THIS BOOK?

This guide lists 500 things you need to know about Tokyo in 100 different categories. Most of these are places to visit, with practical information to help you find your way. Others are bits of information that help you get to know the city and its habitants. The aim of this guide is to inspire, not to cover the city from A to Z.

The places listed in the guide are given an address, including the neighbourhood, and a number. The neighbourhood and number allow you to find the locations on the maps at the beginning of the book: first look for the map of the corresponding neighbourhood, then look for the right number. A word of caution: these maps are not detailed enough to allow you to find specific locations in the city. You can obtain an excellent map from any tourist office or in most hotels. Or the addresses can be located on a smartphone.

Please also bear in mind that cities change all the time. The chef who hits a high note one day may be uninspiring on the day you happen to visit. The hotel ecstatically reviewed in this book might suddenly go downhill under a new manager. The bar considered one of the 5 must-visit bars in Shinjuku Golden-Gai might be empty on the night you visit. This is obviously a highly personal selection. You might not always agree with it. If you want to leave a comment, recommend a bar or reveal your favourite secret place, please visit the website *www.the500hiddensecrets.com* – you'll also find free tips and the latest news about the series there – or follow *@500hiddensecrets* on Instagram or Facebook and leave a comment.

THE AUTHOR

Yukiko Tajima was born and raised in Tokyo. In her mid-20s, she decided she wanted to see another part of the world – not just as a tourist but to live there. And so she moved to the UK. After living there for seven years in the 1990s, she started to rediscover and appreciate her own culture more than ever. Since then she has been involved in many different projects to promote Japanese culture abroad.

Yukiko Tajima now lives in the heart of Tokyo, which is visited by tourists from all over the world throughout the year. As a local, she started wondering whether these tourists have access to all of the available information. Thanks to today's technology, including smartphone apps and online translators, travelling by yourself in a city where you do not understand the language has become much easier, but that still doesn't mean that everyone can find out everything there is to know. That is why Yukiko Tajima wrote this book: she hopes that it will allow people to get to know Tokyo a bit better than they do now. She herself now is, after writing this book, prouder of her city than she ever was.

The author would like to thank all her friends who helped gather the addresses. She also wants to thank Luster Publishers for giving her the opportunity to discover things about Tokyo that she didn't know yet. Last but not least, she thanks Tinne Luyten, because without her, she would never have found out about this excellent series of guidebooks.

N° DISTRICT — Area name

① SHIBUYA-KU — Shibuya

② SHIBUYA-KU / MEGURO-KU — Daikanyama, Ebisu, Hiroo and Nakameguro

③ SHIBUYA-KU — Harajuku

④ MINATO-KU — Aoyama

⑤ MINATO-KU — Akasaka, Yotsuya and Ichigaya

⑥ MINATO-KU — Azabu, Roppongi and Hiroo

⑦ SHINJUKU-KU — Yoyogi and Shinjuku

⑧ CHIYODA-KU / CHUO-KU — Ginza and Nihonbashi

⑨ CHIYODA-KU — Kanda

⑩ BUNKYO-KU / TAITO-KU — Ueno and Asakusa

⑪ TOSHIMA-KU — Ikebukuro and Waseda

⑫ NAKANO-KU / SUGINAMI-KU — Tokyo West

⑬ SETAGAYA-KU — Setagaya

⑭ SHINAGAWA-KU / OTA-KU — Tokyo South

⑮ SUMIDA-KU / KOTO-KU — Tokyo East

TOKYO

overview districts

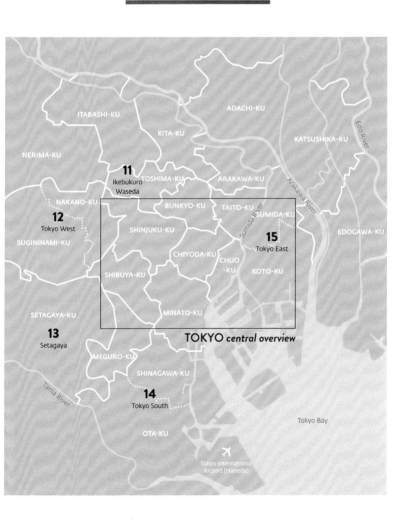

TOKYO

central overview

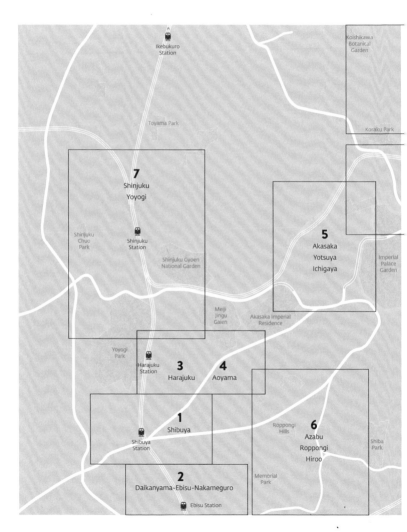

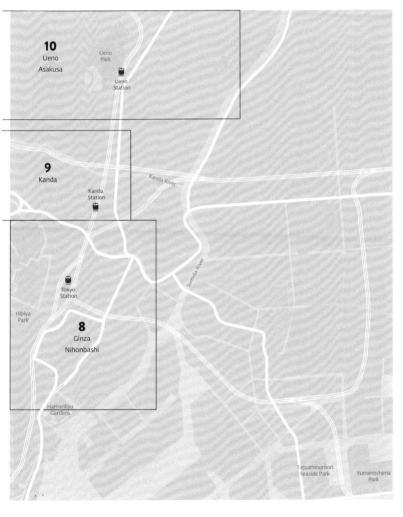

10
Ueno
Asakusa

Ueno
Park

Ueno
Station

9
Kanda

Kanda River

Kanda
Station

Sumida River

Tokyo
Station

Hibiya
Park

8
Ginza
Nihonbashi

Hamarikyu
Gardens

Tatsuminomori
Seaside Park

Yumenoshima
Park

Map 1
SHIBUYA-KU
Shibuya

Shibuya
Hikarie

Map 2
SHIBUYA-KU / MEGURO-KU
Daikanyama, Ebisu, Hiroo and Nakameguro

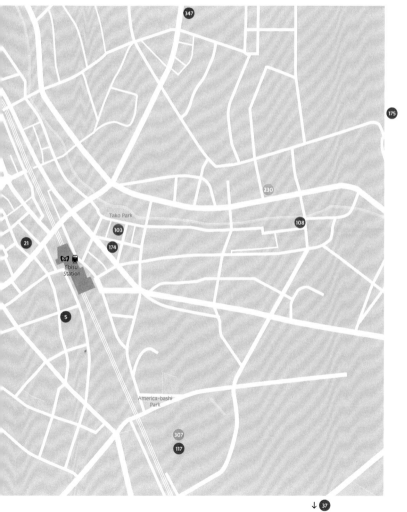

347

175

230

108

Tako Park

103

21

174

Ebisu
Station

5

America-bashi
Park

307

117

↓ 37

EAT — **DRINK** — SHOP — **BUILDINGS** — DISCOVER — **CULTURE** — CHILDREN — SLEEP — **WEEKEND** — RANDOM

Map 3
SHIBUYA-KU
Harajuku

Map 4
MINATO-KU
Aoyama

↑ 451

385
292
447

Akasaka Imperial
Residence

Aoyama-itchōme
Station

115

Gaiemmae
Station

239

Aoyama
Park

211

150
157

201

226

281

182
193

206

288 29
346

352

Nogizaka
Station

Tokyo
Metropolitan
Aoyama Park
South District

189

Map 5
MINATO-KU
Akasaka, Yotsuya and Ichigaya

Map 6

MINATO-KU

Azabu, Roppongi and Hiroo

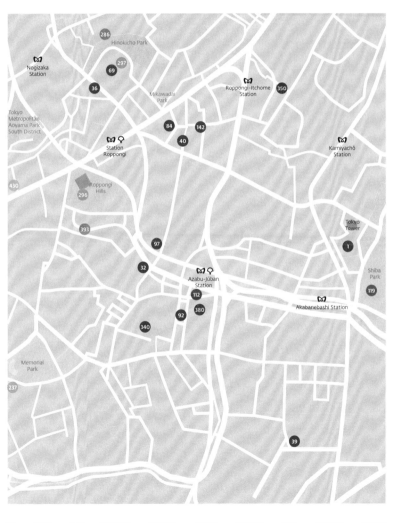

Map 7

SHINJUKU-KU

Yoyogi and Shinjuku

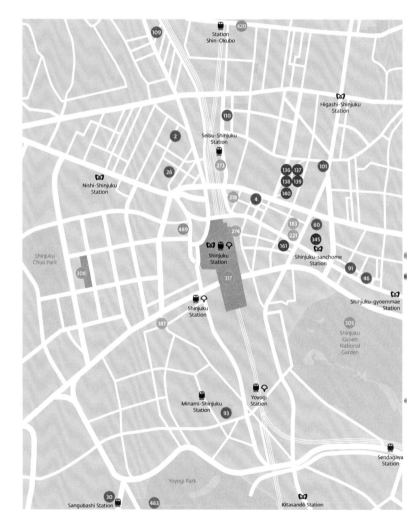

Map 8
CHIYODA-KU / CHUO-KU
Ginza and Nihonbashi

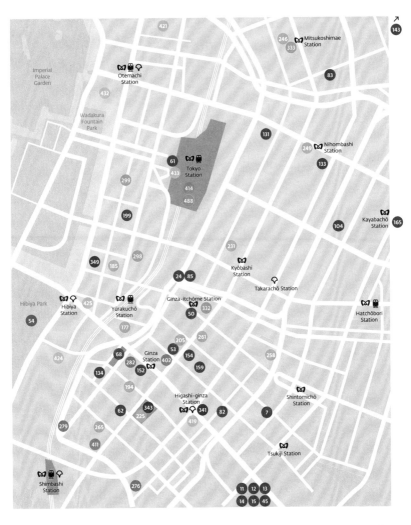

EAT — DRINK — SHOP — BUILDINGS — DISCOVER — **CULTURE** — CHILDREN — SLEEP — **WEEKEND** — RANDOM

Map 9
CHIYODA-KU
Kanda

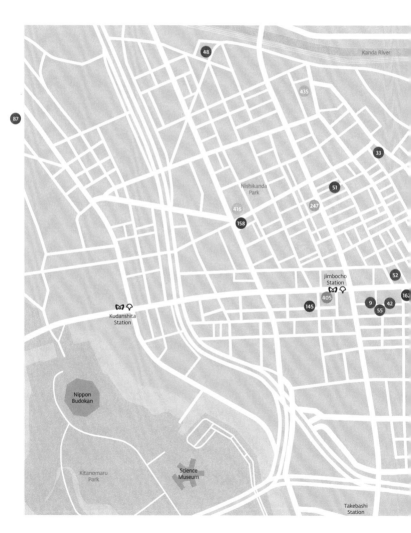

→
143

Map 10

BUNKYO-KU / TAITO-KU

Ueno and Asakusa

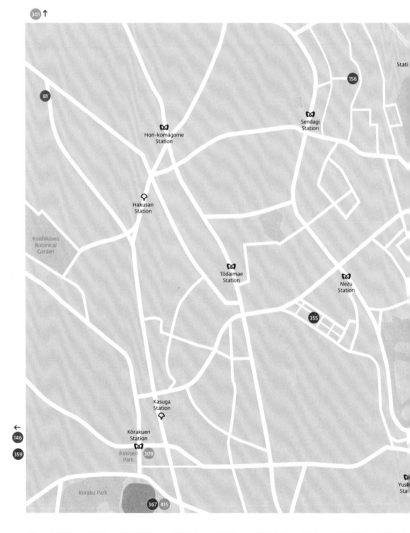

Map 11

TOSHIMA-KU

Ikebukuro and Waseda

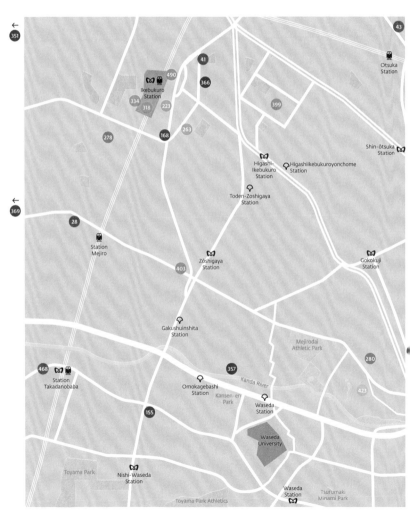

Map 12

NAKANO-KU / SUGINAMI-KU

Tokyo West

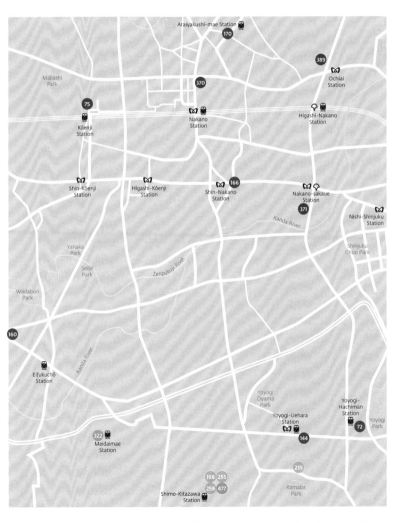

Map 13
SETAGAYA-KU
Setagaya

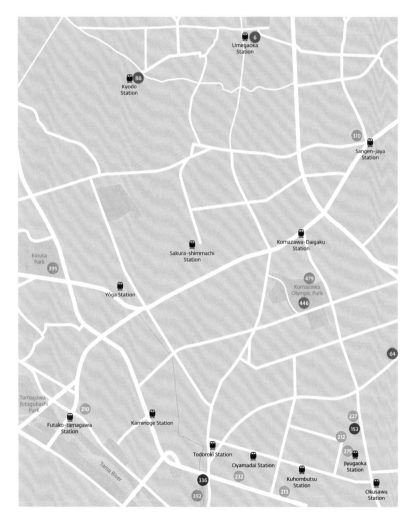

Umegaoka Station 6

Kyodo Station 86

Sangen-jaya Station 310

Komazawa-Daigaku Station

Sakura-shimmachi Station

Kinuta Park 395

Komazawa Olympic Park 479 446

Yōga Station

64

Tamagawa-futagobashi Park

Futako-tamagawa Station 210

Kaminoge Station

227

153

212

Todoroki Station

275

Jiyugaoka Station

Oyamadai Station 232

Kuhombutsu Station

Okusawa Station

Tama River 336 392 213

EAT — **DRINK** — SHOP — **BUILDINGS** — DISCOVER — **CULTURE** — CHILDREN — SLEEP — WEEKEND — RANDOM

Map 14
SHINAGAWA-KU / OTA-KU
Tokyo South

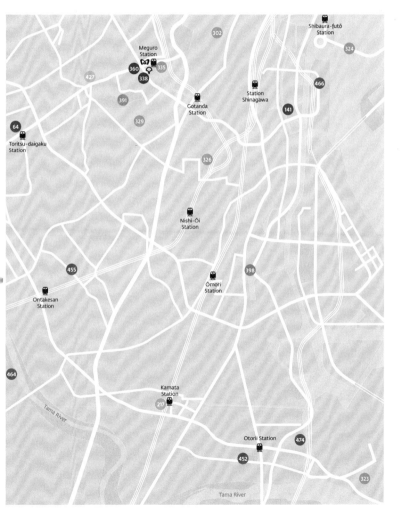

Map 15
SUMIDA-KU / KOTO-KU
Tokyo East

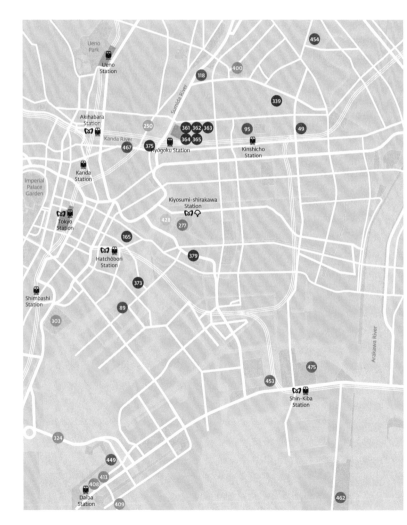

KANDA MATSUYA

120 PLACES TO EAT OR BUY GOOD FOOD

5 great

KAISEKI *and* JAPANESE

restaurants

---

1 **TOFUYA UKAI**
4-4-13 Shiba Koen
Minato-ku ⑥
+81 (0)3-3436-1028
ukai.co.jp

At the foot of Tokyo Tower, you can enjoy a full course tofu meal while gazing at a gorgeous Japanese garden. The tofu served at this restaurant is made in Hachioji, using exquisite water. They also serve a comprehensive selection of sakes that pair nicely with your meal.

2 **KIKUURA**
7-16-3 Nishi-Shinjuku
Shinjuku-ku ⑦
+81 (0)3-5389-5581
kikuura.com

A small restaurant that serves superb meals at reasonable prices. If you go there at lunch, you can also order *donburi* (a bowl of rice with a topping) at an even more reasonable price. Bag a seat at the counter so you can watch the chef at work in the open kitchen.

3 **KANETANAKA**
AT: CERULEAN TOWER TOKYU HOTEL
26-1 Sakuragaokacho
Shibuya-ku ①
+81 (0)3-3476-3420
kanetanaka.co.jp

There are two restaurants in the Cerulean Tower. The one in the basement occupies a 50-square-metre room that overlooks the Noh theatre. They only accept groups of two to sixteen people every evening (two groups for lunch). The other one, Kanetanaka-so, is on the second floor, and serves breakfast, lunch, and dinner.

4 KURUMAYA BEKKAN

3-21-1 Shinjuku
Shinjuku-ku ⑦
+81 (0)3-3352-5566
kuruma-ya.co.jp

This restaurant used to be a salon for authors during the Showa Period. On the ground floor, they serve *teppanyaki*. *Sukiyaki* (beef and vegetables cooked in soy sauce, sake, and sugar), *shabu shabu* (thinly-sliced beef and vegetables boiled in water) and other Japanese dishes are served upstairs.

5 KUON

1-14-15 Ebisu-Minami
Shibuya-ku ②
+81 (0)3-3793-1319
ku-on.com

A quiet and cosy restaurant on a back street in this busy area. It may also be the perfect place to celebrate your anniversary as the price/quality ratio of their meals is outstanding. They also have an *à la carte* menu (*a-ra-ka-ru-to* in Japanese) that changes every month.

1 TOFUYA UKAI

5

INEXPENSIVE SUSHI

restaurants

---

6 **SUSHI NO MIDORI**
1-20-7 Umegaoka
Setagaya-ku ⑬
+81 (0)3-3429-0066
sushinomidori.co.jp

One of the most popular sushi restaurants in Tokyo, with branches in Shibuya, Ginza and other locations. Their signature *Ganso Anago* is a whole conger eel on top of rice. You can check in online so you can go shopping while waiting for your turn instead of having to queue.

7 **TSUKIJI TAMA SUSHI**
1-9-4 Tsukiji
Chuo-ku ⑧
+81 (0)3-3541-1917
tamasushi.co.jp

Since this place opened in Tsukiji in 1924, they have always had a reputation for quality sushi and service. At lunchtime, you can enjoy a set sushi menu, a bowl of Tsukiji-don, or *chirashi-sushi* at a reasonable price. Their Ginza branch (5-8-20 Ginza, Chuo-ku) offers *tabe hodai* (eat all you can) if you have a large appetite.

8 **TSUKIJI BIG SUSHI**
1-10-1 Otowa
Bunkyo-ku ⑪
+81 (0)3-3945-2361

Though their name refers to 'Tsukiji', they are not actually located in Tsukiji. But each piece of sushi is as big as their name suggests. Here you can enjoy superb sushi for the price of *kaiten sushi* (conveyor belt sushi). You'll definitely feel full after their hearty lunch.

9 **ROPPO SUSHI**
   1-11-8 Kanda Jinbocho
   Chiyoda-ku ⑨
   +81 (0)3-3291-6879

This small restaurant is located near Jinbocho subway station. You can watch the chefs at work while you are waiting and eating. The pickles they serve in-between dishes are equally delicious. They only have 12 seats at the counter, so it can get very busy here very quickly.

10 **468**
   3-23-14 Nishi-Asakusa
   Taito-ku ⑩
   +81 (0)3-3843-6964

Their name is pronounced as 'yoroppa', which is the Japanese word for 'Europe'. This small sushi restaurant has only six seats and serves *bo-sushi* or 'loaf' sushi. This is prepared by layering fish and rice in a long, thin wooden box. You can also order takeaway by phone.

The 5 best places in
TSUKIJI MARKET

11 **SUSHI DAI**
6-21-2 Tsukiji
Chuo-ku ⑧
+81 (0)3-3541-3738
tsukiji-sushidai.com

Here they source their fish straight from the fish market. They are also very particular about the soy sauce and salt they use, carefully choosing the types that they believe are most suitable for sushi. From Monday till Saturday, they are open until 4 am. Credit cards accepted, but not during lunch.

12 **TSUKIJI DONBURI ICHIBA**
4-9-5 Tsukiji
Chuo-ku ⑧
+81 (0)3-3541-8978

While *Donburi* means 'bowl', it often refers to a bowl of cooked rice topped with something. Popular dishes here include *Ichiba-don*, aka Market don, with sashimi on top, and *Maguro no hohoniku-don*, with grilled tuna cheek. On some weekdays, they are open 24 hours.

13 **YAJIMA**
Tsukiji Oroshiuri Shijo 8 Gokan
5-2-1 Tsukiji
Chuo-ku ⑧
+81 (0)3-3541-0729
tsukijigourmet.or.jp

Yajima is a popular ramen place with the people who work in Tsukiji Market. They serve a speciality, called Oyster Ramen, from October until March. You can choose between salt (*shio*) or miso ramen. Don't forget to order homemade 'Jumbo' *gyoza* (Chinese dumpling).

14 HIGASHI INDO KARE SHOKAI

4-10-7 Tsukiji
Chuo-ku ⑧
+81 (0)3-3545-5108

Most people visit Tsukiji to eat sushi or sashimi. If you're not that keen on raw fish however, why not give Japanese-style curry a try? As well as curry and rice, they invented *curry onigiri*, or rice balls made of rice cooked with curry sauce.

15 KANNO

4-9-5 Tsukiji
Chuo-ku ⑧
+81 (0)3-3541-9291

Another shop that serves rice bowls. Their prices have remained unchanged since they opened, so if you are looking for some affordable nosh (most of the restaurants in Tsukiji are relatively inexpensive), then try this place. Their signature dish is *Sanshu-mori*, or rice topped with tuna, salmon roe, and sea urchin.

5 things you need to know
BEFORE
EATING SUSHI

---

16 **EDO-MAE STYLE**

There are several styles of sushi. The *Edo-mae* style (Tokyo-style) – with raw fish scattered on top of rice – is probably the style that is most widely known as sushi outside of Japan. *Edokko* (a Japanese term referring to people born and raised in Edo, or Tokyo) tend to be impatient. So, this style suits them to a tee as the rice and fish can be eaten at the same time.

17 **GARI**

Gari is thinly-sliced pickled ginger. It has an antimicrobial effect, so it may prevent us from having food poisoning. It is used to cleanse the palate between eating different pieces of sushi. The word *gari* is only used for sushi ginger. The proper Japanese word for ginger is *shoga*.

18 **USE YOUR FINGERS**

Eating *Edo-mae* style sushi the proper way means you should use your fingers, not chopsticks. Grab your sushi with your thumb, index and middle fingers, turn it upside down, dip the fish into the soy sauce and eat it in one go.

19 **HOW TO ORDER**

You should start by ordering something light, like plaice or another white fish or squid, and then oily fish, like tuna or conger eel. Ultimately, you can order whatever you feel like. If you start with oily fish, you can cleanse your palate with some *gari* and green tea.

20 **DON'T WEAR PERFUME**

If you decide to go to a proper sushi restaurant – not the conveyer belt type – then don't wear perfume or only dab on the tiniest amount. The scent of perfume can easily spoil sushi. This rule also applies to other places, like sake bars for example.

18 USE YOUR FINGERS

The 5 best restaurants for
REGIONAL CUISINE

---

21 **ATERUI**
1-8-10 Ebisu-Nishi
Shibuya-ku ②
+81 (0)3-5784-2668
aterui-ebisu.jimdo.com

The owner sources all his fresh ingredients directly from Hokkaido, where he was born. A variety of fish, sea urchin, oyster, Chinese mitten crab … everything they serve is very different from what you can eat at other *izakaya* (bars). If you are lucky, you might come across some dishes that are rarely available in Tokyo.

22 **HONKE ABEYA**
3-2-40 Kagurazaka
Shinjuku-ku ⑤
+81 (0)3-5225-2664
honkeabeya.com

Here you can eat *Hinai-Jidori*, or the chicken they raise in Akita and which is considered to be one of the top three chicken breeds. Their *Oyako-don*, or chicken and egg bowl, comes highly recommended. As Akita is a rice-producing area, it also produces good sake, which you can, of course, taste here.

23 **YANMO**
5-5-25 Minami-Aoyama
Minato-ku ④
+81 (0)3-5466-0636
yanmo.co.jp

From sashimi to grilled fish, this place serves fish from the Izu Peninsula, Shizuoka. During the lunch hour, your fish is served with a bowl of rice, miso soup, and a side dish, all of which are delicious. All you can eat!

24 **TOSA DINING OKYAKU**
AT: GINZA TOWER, 2ND FL.
1-3-13 Ginza
Chuo-ku ⑧
+81 (0)3-3538-4351
marugotokochi.com/shop/
okyaku.html

There are many *antena shoppu* (shops that sell the specialities of a particular prefecture) in Ginza. This restaurant is in Kochi's shop and serves the regional dishes of Kochi, a prefecture that has plenty of seafood. Enjoy *katsuo no tataki* (lightly-broiled skipjack tuna). They also have delicious pork and beef dishes.

25 **D47 SHOKUDO**
AT: HIKARIE BUILDING, 8TH FL.
2-21-1 Shibuya
Shibuya-ku ①
+81 (0)3-6427-2303
d-department.com

In Japan, there are 47 prefectures. You can enjoy specialities from all over the country at this restaurant. They have a variety of *teishoku* (set menus) that change every month. They regularly organise food-related events and workshops so you can learn more about regional cuisine.

The 5 best places for
TEMPURA

---

26 **TENHIDE**
7-12-21 Nishi-Shinjuku
Shinjuku-ku ⑦
+81 (0)3-5386-3630
ten-hide.com

This restaurant is located on a quiet street, and is just a seven-minute walk from busy Shinnku Station. They source the best seasonal ingredients from Tsukiji Market every day for their traditional Edo-style dishes. In the evening, they only serve set menus, so go at lunch time if you just want to sample their tempura.

27 **YAMANOUE**
AT: HILLTOP HOTEL
1-1 Surugadai Kanda
Chiyoda-ku ⑨
+81 (0)3-3293-2831
yamanoue-hotel.co.jp/
restaurant/tempura/

A posh restaurant in the Hilltop Hotel (in Japanese, *Yamanoue Hotel*) where many famous literary figures, such as Yukio Mishima and Yasunari Kawabata, stayed to write their novels. Don't miss their *Maruju*, a tempura of thick-cut sweet potato. We recommend sharing though because this is a big dish.

28 **TENSAKU**
3-2-16 Shimo-Ochiai
Shinjuku-ku ⑪
+81 (0)3-3954-1036

A popular tempura restaurant near Mejiro Station. They also serve unusual tempura, in addition to shrimp and vegetable. This depends on the seasons, of course, when sea urchin, crab, fig, *mochi* (rice cake) and baby corn are available. The friendly atmosphere makes you feel very welcome.

29 MIYAKAWA

6-1-6 Minami-Aoyama
Minato-ku ④
+81 (0)3-3400-3722

A small Kansai-style tempura restaurant on the opposite side of the Nezu Museum. In Kanto, an egg is added to the batter whereas they don't usually do this in Kansai. The prawns, scallop, aubergine, and other seasonal ingredients in the thin batter are very crispy. Like so many other tempura restaurants, the lunch is very reasonable in price.

30 KIKUYA

4-6-1 Ebisu
Shibuya-ku ⑦
+81 (0)3-5422-9077
kikuyajp.com

A casual standing bar where you can enjoy tempura and drinks, where you'll run into men and women of all ages. They have some unconventional tempura that you probably can't find in other restaurants, such as coriander, *natto* (fermented soybeans), *beni shoga* (red pickled ginger), and *takoyaki* (ball-shaped battered octopus).

27 YAMANOUE

The 5 best places for
JAPANESE NOODLES

---

31 KANDA MATSUYA
1-13 Kanda-Sudacho
Chiyoda-ku ⑨
+81 (0)3-3251-1556
kanda-matsuya.jp

They have been serving hand-kneaded *soba* (buckwheat noodle) here since the Meiji period. *Goma* (sesame) *soba* is the owner's recommended menu and also the most popular one for women. The *sobagaki* (a dumpling made of buckwheat and water) and *Ten-Nanban* (tempura soba) are also very good.

32 SARASHINA HORII
3-11-4 Moto-Azabu
Minato-ku ⑥
+81 (0)3-3403-3401
sarashina-horii.com

This restaurant is said to have opened over 200 years ago. Their signature menu of *Sarashina Soba* consists of white noodles that are made of buckwheat kernels. The seasonal soba is prepared with *Sarashina Soba* mixed with an ingredient. You can also choose between two types of dipping sauces.

33 MATSUO
2-1-7 Sarugaku-cho
Chiyoda-ku ⑨
+81 (0)3-3291-3529

The menu has plenty of options but if you can't decide then order *Nishoku-mori*, or two different flavours on one plate. They also have a variety of side dishes, including tempura and *yaki-miso* (grilled miso). Try *sobagaki* with red bean paste if you still have some room for dessert.

31 KANDA MATSUYA

34 **KYOURAKUTEI**
3-6 Kagurazaka
Shinjuku-ku ⑤
+81 (0)3-3269-3233
kyourakutei.com

Located off Kagurazaka. The noodles here are made of stone-ground buckwheat and are very popular with *soba* fanatics. Their *Zaru Soba* are prepared with 100% buckwheat, without wheat flour, making them a good option for anyone on a gluten-free diet. They also serve a wide selection of sakes. Have some with a stewed beef tendon.

35 **GONBEE**
5-9-3 Minami-Aoyama
Minato-ku ③
+81 (0)3-3406-5733
smoke-stone.com/gonbee

This place opened in 1976 and they have stuck with their style, despite the fact that other shops in the neighbourhood have come and gone. Although they are situated in one of the most expensive areas in Tokyo, their set lunch menus are very affordable. In the evening, you can order snack portions of their dishes to go with your sake.

5 great places for
RAMEN

---

36 **TENHO**
   7-8-5 Roppongi
   Minato-ku ⑥
   +81 (0)3-3404-6155

Located in a building in front of Tokyo Midtown. The noodles of their '1-3-5 Ramen' are chewier, and their soy sauce-based soup is oilier and saltier. *Menbari* is an alternative version of their 1-3-5 Ramen with an even tougher noodle. Once you taste it, you might find it highly addictive however.

37 **ISHIN**
   3-4-1 Kami-Osaki
   Meguro-ku ②
   +81 (0)3-3444-8480

If you are not that keen on oily and fatty foods but want to eat ramen, then this is the place for you. Their soup is clear in colour but has a good texture, and you will find that you simply cannot resist having it all. Don't forget to sample their *wonton* (Chinese dumpling)!

38 **MENYA NUKAJI**
   3-12 Udagawacho
   Shibuya-ku ①
   +81 (0)3-3476-8148

They serve both ramen and *tukemen* (dipping noodles). Their soup is a mixture of meat broth and fish broth – thick but not too heavy. If you are in Tokyo in the summer, then try their *Katsuo-dashi no Hiyashi Niku Soba* (meat noodles in a cold bonito soup).

39 RAMEN JIRO
2-16-4 Mita
Minato-ku ⑥

Ramen Jiro is a cult restaurant among ramen lovers. Memorise a few Japanese words before going so you can customise your order, such as *nin-niku* (garlic), *yasai* (vegetable), and *karame* (thicker soup), *abura* (oil), and *sono mama* (without topping). Their portions tend to be substantial, so you can order a smaller portion if you wish.

40 SHIJIMI RAMEN
3-15-25 Roppongi
Minato-ku ⑥
+81 (0)3-6804-2081

This place does not look like a ramen shop at all with its black decoration scheme. Their soup is made of *shijimi* (freshwater clams) and is supposed to prevent a hangover after a night of heavy drinking. Eat up all the soup as it is good for your health.

The 5 best places for
ONIGIRI
(rice balls)

---

41 NEKASE GENMAI IROHA
Wacca Ikebukuro
1-8-1 Higashi-Ikebukuro
Toshima-ku ⑪
+81 (0)70-6469-4168
omusubi-iroha.com

Nekase genmai is sprouted brown rice. Like ordinary brown rice it is very nutritious, but it is softer and therefore easier to chew, even for small children. They combine it with a variety of ingredients, from pickled plums and salmon to cream cheese with *mentaiko* (spicy cod roe) and pork *kakuni* (braised pork).

42 ONIGIRI NO KOBAYASHI
1-5 Kanda-Jinbocho
Chiyoda-ku ⑨
+81 (0)3-3291-9293

A friendly shop on Suzuran Street. Their *onigiri* remind Japanese people of their mother's. The shop is crowded with people who work nearby as you can take out or eat in. If your favourite option is sold out then just ask anyway – they might make another one for you.

43 ONIGIRI BONGO
2-26-3 Kita-Otsuka
Toshima-ku ⑪
+81 (0)3-3910-5617
onigiribongo.info

Here you can sit at the counter, like in a sushi shop, and order what you like. They then prepare it for you and you can eat fresh *onigiri*, that is still warm. Choose from over 50 toppings. Pay an additional 50 yen to have two toppings on a piece of *onigiri*.

44 ONIGIRI ASAKUSA YADOROKU

**3-9-10 Asakusa
Taito-ku ⑩
+81 (0)3-3874-1615
*onigiriyadoroku.com***

This is the oldest *onigiri* shop in Tokyo. They source their rice and ingredients from all over Japan. You can eat your *onigiri* inside the shop with a bowl of tasty miso soup or take out your meal. You can order by the piece, so why not have some *onigiri* as a snack? Simple but satisfying.

45 ONIGIRIYA MARUTOYO

**4-9-9 Tsukiji
Chuo-ku ⑧
+81 (0)3-3541-6010**

A reputable shop in Tsukiji Market. They have a great selection – from traditional *onigiri*, such as salmon and pickled plums, to more unusual options, such as *ebi-furai* (deep fried prawn). Do try their *Oyako* (meaning parent and child, in this case, salmon and salmon roe).

44 ONIGIRI ASAKUSA YADOROKU

5 great
GYOZA RESTAURANTS

---

46 **GYOZA NO FUKUHO**
2-8-6 Shinjuku
Shinjuku-ku ⑦
+81 (0)3-5367-1582
fukuho.net

People are always queueing here. They have two types of *gyoza*, *yaki gyoza* (grilled) and *sui gyoza* (boiled), both of which contain plenty of vegetables, making this a healthy option. The former is crispy, while the latter one has a *mochi*-like texture – soft and squishy.

47 **HARAJUKU GYOZARO**
6-2-4 Jingumae
Shibuya-ku ③
+81 (0)3-3406-4743

Despite its location, this place is not that expensive, which is why it is always crowded. They serve two types of *gyoza*: *yaki gyoza* and *sui gyoza*, with or without *nin-niku* (garlic) and *nira* (Chinese chive). Try the crispy grilled gyoza which contain a lot of meat juice.

48 **FUJIIYA**
2-21-11 Misakicho
Chiyoda-ku ⑨
+81 (0)3-3239-8295

In addition to traditional *gyoza* (which they call 'Ganso Gyoza'), they also serve *Ebi Nira* (prawn and Chinese chive) *Gyoza*, *Pari Pari* (crispy) *Gyoza*, *Shiso* (Japanese basil) *Gyoza*, and much more. Make life easy and just order *Zenpin Moriawase* – four different types of grilled gyoza on the same plate.

49 KAMEIDO GYOZA HONTEN

5-3-4 Kameido
Koto-ku ⑮
+81 (0)3-3681-8854

Their menu is as straightforward as it gets because they only serve *gyoza* here. As soon as you order a drink, the freshly-grilled *gyoza* is brought to your table. There are five pieces to a plate, and you have to eat at least ten. But don't worry; their *gyoza* are not that filling. You will find that you can easily gobble up that second plate, and order more.

50 GINZA TENRYU

AT: PUZZLE GINZA, 4TH FL.
2-15-19 Ginza
Chuo-ku ⑧
+81 (0)3-3561-3543
ginza-tenryu.com

Their *gyoza*, which are made according to their own recipe since the 1940s, are huge. Don't worry about garlic breath after eating here because the dishes don't contain any flavouring ingredients. In addition to *gyoza*, they serve authentic Pekinese cuisine.

The 5 best places to eat
JAPANESE-STYLE CURRY

---

51   RICE CURRY MANTEN
1-54 Kanda-Jinbocho
Chiyoda-ku ⑨
+81 (0)3-3291-3274

There are more than 30 curry shops in Jinbocho. Manten is one of the more affordable ones in the area. *Katsu* (deep-fried pork cutlet) and *korokke* (croquette) are the two most popular toppings. If you are super-hungry, order a *Zenbu-Nose* (an everything curry) – you can have *katsu*, *korroke*, sausage and *gyoza* all in one go!

52   KYOEIDO
1-6 Kanda-Jinbocho
Chiyoda-ku ⑨
+81 (0)3-3291-1475
kyoueidoo.com

This restaurant opened in 1924. The chef introduced Sumatran-style curry to Japan (but he tweaked the recipe a bit so the Japanese would really love it). From October until April, they serve baked apples with a dollop of fresh cream. Don't miss out as they only prepare 25-30 portions a day.

53   GRILL SWISS
3-5-16 Ginza
Chuo-ku ⑧
+81 (0)3-3563-3206
*ginza-swiss.com/
bar-and-grill/*

This was the first shop to serve *katsu* curry. Their curry sauce, which tastes delicious with the cutlet, is made using various vegetables and fruit, including onion, carrot, and apple. You can order a *hire-katsu* (deep-fried pork fillet) curry sandwich and curry rice to take away.

54 MATSUMOTORO

1-2 Hibiya Koen
Chiyoda-ku ⑧
+81 (0)3-3503-1451
matsumotoro.co.jp

When Hibiya Park, the first Western-style park in Japan, opened in 1903, this restaurant opened at the same time, in the park. As it was very sophisticated and stylish, many artists and authors, including Soseki Natsume, loved eating curry rice and having a coffee here. Enjoy your curry and the lovely view!

55 KITCHEN NANKAI

1-5 Kanda-Jinbocho
Chiyoda-ku ⑨
+81 (0)3-3292-0036

Another shop in Jinbocho. Their most popular dish is *katsu* curry, but their just-fried cutlet comes in a darkish curry, verging on black. Around lunch, there is always a queue of *sarari man* (office workers) who need an energy boost for the afternoon.

55 KITCHEN NANKAI

5 must-visit restaurants for
MEAT LOVERS

---

56 **TORI CHATARO**
7-12 Uguisudanicho
Shibuya-ku ①
+81 (0)3-6416-0364

As this place is far from the centre of Shibuya, this yakitori restaurant is a real hidden gem. Yakitori places tend to be noisy, but this one is a little more sophisticated. Enjoy excellent chicken while listening to hits from the last century (probably the chef's favourite genre).

57 **REBAYA**
AT: KR BUILDING, 1ST FL.
1-22-12 Yotsuya
Shinjuku-ku ⑤
+81 (0)3-6380-4988

There are several good *izakaya* on Shinmichi-dori in Yotsuya. This yakitori place serves some special options, including *chochin* (egg), *saezuri* (throat), and *shiro reba* (white liver). Limited availability, so I recommend going there early in the evening.

58 **HAGAKURE**
2-8-11 Shibuya
Shibuya-ku ①
+81 (0)3-6416-0364

Located on the upper floor of an old building between Shibuya and Omotesando. This place serves *Yakiton* (grilled pork). Don't worry if you don't know what to order – just say *omakase* (which means 'you decide for me'). Be careful not to drink too much, or you might fall down the stairs on the way out.

59 SANBYAKUYA

12-4 Shinsencho
Shibuya-ku ①
+81 (0)3-3477-1129
sanbyakuya.com

Shinsen is located within walking distance from Shibuya and is one of the up and coming areas where there are many excellent restaurants. At Sanbyakuya, they start by serving you a pile of shredded cabbage, which you should eat in between meat dishes. As you may know, cabbage promotes good digestion.

60 SHINJUKU HORUMON

3-12-3 Shinjuku
Shinjuku-ku ⑦
+81 (0)3-3353-4129
ishii-world.jp/shinjuku-horumon

Horumon-yaki, grilled beef and pork offal, is an excellent way to consume mineral and collagen and the Japanese love it. They also serve other cuts you might be more familiar with, such as tripe or skirt steak. Their retro-style interiors will make you feel as if you have travelled back in time to the Showa period.

60 SHINJUKU HORUMON

The 5 best shops for
SHAVED ICE

---

61 TORAYA TOKYO
AT: THE TOKYO STATION
HOTEL, 2ND FL.
1-9-1 Marunouchi
Chiyoda-ku ⑧
+81 (0)3-5220-2345
toraya-group.co.jp

Toraya is one of the oldest Japanese confectionery shops and is said to have opened in the late Muromachi era (in the 16th century!). They usually start serving shaved ice from late spring until September. Their original ginger syrups can work miracles, energising any tired body.

62 SANTOKUDO
7-8-19 Ginza
Chuo-ku ⑧
+81 (0)3-3289-3131
santokudo.jp

This black tea speciality shop serves Taiwanese-style shaved ice in summer. Do try the one with Taiwan's best quality apple mango. You may be surprised at first as the ice is literally covered in mango chunks but they cut up a whole mango for each serving!

63 NANIWAYA
2-12-4 Asakusa
Taito-ku ⑩
+81 (0)3-3842-0988
a-naniwaya.com

This is actually a *tai-yaki* (fish-shaped cake) shop but they also serve shaved ice in summer. Asayake (meaning 'dawn'), which comes with toppings of red bean paste, milk, and strawberry sauce, is the most delightful flavour combo. The homemade seasonal fruit syrups are equally delicious.

64 **CHIMOTO**
1-4-6 Yakumo
Meguro-ku ⑬⑭
+81 (0)3-3718-4643

In summer you'll often see a queue here at opening time when the locals queue for their famous shaved ice. When you are finally seated, just order *omakase*, which literally means 'you decide for me'. *Kakigori* resembles a tiny mountain of ice that is topped with *matcha* syrup. It is quite similar to a snow cone. As you dig in, you'll discover *mochi* pieces, chestnuts and jellies at the bottom.

65 **RYAN**
7 Arakicho
Shinjuku-ku ⑦
twitter.com/arakicho_kori

A bar off the street that only serves shaved ice in the afternoon in summer and autumn. Their syrups, which are made with seasonal fruit, are delicious when used as a topping on the airy, soft pieces of ice. You can order *aigake* (half and half) for a taste of two types of syrup. Check their Twitter for more information.

64 CHIMOTO

5 superb
ICE-CREAM
parlours

---

66 **PARIYA**
AT: TOKYU FOODSHOW
2-24-1 Shibuya
Shibuya-ku ①
+81 (0)3-3477-4828
pariya.jp

A gelato shop in Tokyu Foodshow, located in the basement of Tokyu Department Store and Mark City. They have a selection of Japanese flavours including *matcha*, *murasaki-imo* (purple sweet potato), *kabocha* pumpkin, and *hoji-cha* (roasted green tea). The shop also sells a variety of deli items for your *bento* (packed lunch).

67 **SILKREAM**
AT: HAIMANTEN JINNAN
BUILDING, 1ST FL.
1-19-3 Jinnan
Shibuya-ku ①
+81 (0)3-3464-4900
nissei-com.co.jp/silkream

Sofuto crimu, or soft serve ice cream, is very popular in Japan. It is usually served in a cone-shaped wafer, but here it comes in a cone made of a thin biscuit. Their ice cream is thick – containing 12.5% fat – and is made using milk from Hokkaido, which is known for its dairy industry.

68 **HANDELS VÄGEN**
AT: TOKYU PLAZA GINZA
5-2-1 Ginza
Chuo-ku ⑧
+81 (0)3-3575-5300
handelsvagen.com

The concept of this shop is 'Kyoto Premium'. Their products are created by a chef who was trained at a Japanese restaurant in Kyoto. He tries to make the best use of seasonal fruit, vegetables, and nuts, mixing a thick ice cream without any food essences or additives.

69 **PALETAS**

Tokyo Midtown Galleria
9-7-3 Akasaka
Minato-ku ⑥
+81 (0)3-6447-4445
paletas.jp

Go here for their ice lollies made of fruit juice, gelato, and yoghurt with fresh fruits and vegetables. They have over 20 flavours, and some of them are typically Japanese, such as Kuri-Matcha (chestnut and green tea) and Kaki Hojicha (*kaki* persimmon and roasted green tea).

70 **MITSUBACHI**

3-38-10 Yushima
Bunkyo-ku ⑩
+81 (0)3-3831-3083
mitsubachi-co.com

This 100-year-old shop in Yushima serves a Japanese-style ice cream called *Ogura aisu*, which is made of red bean paste. If you are more adventurous, then order some *Ogura aisu* like the locals – such as *Ogura anmitsu* (agar jelly topped with ice cream and syrup) or *Ogura shiratama* (mochi balls topped with ice cream)

The 5 best
BAKERIES

---

71 VIRON
33-8 Udagawa-cho
Shibuya-ku ①
+81 (0)3-5458-1776

Their baguette, made with proper French flour, is considered unrivalled in Japan. They have a dining room above the bakery which opens at 9 am. As Viron is located near Tokyu Department's flagship store, it is the perfect place for breakfast before you go shopping or to the cinema or a museum.

72 365 NICHI
1-16-12 Tomigaya
Shibuya-ku ⑫
+81 (0)3-6804-7357

The owner and chef's policy is to bake bread without food additives, only using flour that is produced in Japan. As the shop's name, which means 365 days, suggests, you can buy fresh bread here every day. There is an eat-in space where you can sample of the bread straight from the oven, with a good cup of coffee.

73 BREAD, ESPRESSO &
3-4-9 Jingumae
Shibuya-ku ③
+81 (0)3-5410-2040
bread-espresso.jp

The owner wanted to create an Italian-style bar where people drop in every day. They open at 8 am and by lunchtime and on weekends the place is packed. Their *pain perdu* made with their signature 'Mou' (French for soft) bread is too good for words.

74 **SORA TO MUGI TO**
  2-10-7 Ebisu-Nishi
  Shibuya-ku ②
  +81 (0)3-6427-0158
  soratomugito.com

The owner grows his own organic wheat in Yamanashi to mill his own flour. Then he rigorously selects only the best ingredients for his delicious bread. Try his *Kuromame Pan*, the locals' favourite bread, with sweet black beans and pumpkin.

75 **SHIGEKUNIYA 55
  BAKERY**
  3-22-9 Koenji-Kita
  Suginami-ku ⑫
  +81 (0)3-5356-7617

This bakery originally opened in Kichijoji, became a popular fixture at the UNU Farmer's Market, and moved to the current location in 2014. They take their bread very seriously here as you can tell from the display. Try their tasty savour and sweet bagels for something really good.

75 SHIGEKUNIYA 55 BAKERY

5
JAPANESE SNACKS
you should try

---

76 KREPU

Although it was inspired by a French pancake crêpe, *krepu* was originally created in Harajuku, Japan in the 1970s and has since become a typical sweet of the area. *Krepu* is a piece of pancake folded into four and topped with whipped cream and fruit, or even some chocolate sauce.

77 YAKIIMO

Sweet potatoes baked in a stone oven. From late autumn onwards, you'll often come across food trucks which serve them. Many locals cannot resist the lure of the drivers' call, especially on a cold day. The cooks will often give you a tiny piece to taste, so why not try it?

78 IMAGAWA-YAKI

A small thick pancake filled with *an* (red bean paste). Sometimes also called *kaiten yaki* or *oban-yaki* depending on the region. These days you can take your pick from a wide range of fillings, including custard cream, chocolate cream, cheese cream, and so on. Eat while warm.

79 **TAI-YAKI**

Very similar in taste to *imagawa-yaki*, but *tai-yaki* is baked in a fish-shaped mould, is crispier than *imagawa-yaki* and contains more bean paste. Some of the shops sell *hane tsuki tai-yaki*, with a crispy coating.

80 **TAKO-YAKI**

Tako (octopus) + *yaki* (grill). Octopus mixed in a batter, made with flour, eggs and milk, served with pickled ginger and spring onion. Usually they will serve you six or eight balls on a plate with mayonnaise and *ao nori* (seaweed). Be careful not to burn your tongue.

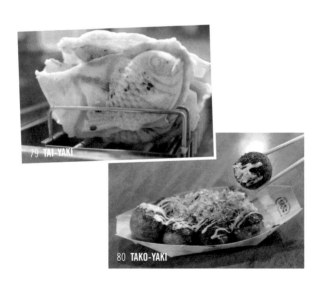

79 TAI-YAKI

80 TAKO-YAKI

5 places to eat
EGG DISHES

---

81 KISABURO NOJO
1-23-11 Sengoku
Bunkyo-ku ⑩
+81 (0)3-3943-3746
kisaburou-sengoku.com

Japanese people love *tamago kake ghan* (cooked rice topped with a raw egg). Don't be deterred by the raw egg however. Here they only use the freshest, best-quality eggs from a trusted source. Add a dash of soy sauce, which is specially produced for them, and you will understand why Japanese people always come back for more.

82 KISSA YOU
4-13-17 Ginza
Chuo-ku ⑧
+81 (0)3-6226-0482
kissa-you.com

A nice old *kissaten* (cafe) near Kabuki-za Theatre, which is famous for its *omuraisu*. The word *omuraisu* comes from 'omelette' with 'rice', or flavoured rice wrapped in or topped with an omelette. Although they have other dishes on the menu, most of the customers tend to order the special.

**83 KYO NO CHISO
HANNARIYA**
AT: UNO BUILDING, 2ND FL.
1-11-15 Nihonbashi
Muromachi
Chuo-ku ⑧
+81 (0)3-3245-1233
hannariya.jp

While the Tokyo-style Japanese omelette contains sugar, its Kyoto sibling is called *dashi-maki* and is made without sugar. This restaurant serves Kyoto cuisine, and most of the lunch menu comes with a piece of *dashi-maki*, which has a delicate and fluffy texture.

84 **YAKITORI MOE**
   3-8-12 Roppongi
   Minato-ku ⑥
   +81 (0)3-5414-1141

Many Japanese people eat rice dishes at the end of their meal at an *izakaya*. At this *yakitori* restaurant, customers usually order *oyako-don* (which literally translates as 'parent and child bowl' because it contains chicken and egg). Their *oyako-don* and chicken broth are so good that you could probably eat this every day.

85 **CENTRE THE BAKERY**
   1-2-1 Ginza
   Chuo-ku ⑧
   +81 (0)3-3562-1016

This bakery specialises in *pain de mie* (a type of rectangular loaf), but they also serve sandwiches using their bread – they use different types of bread depending on the filling. Their *Omuretsu Sando* (egg omelette sandwich) is a sandwich with a just-cooked omelette that almost melts in your mouth.

85 CENTRE THE BAKERY

The 5 best places for
OKONOMIYAKI
and MONJAYAKI

---

86 HASSHO
1-21-18 Kyodo
Setagaya-ku ⑬
+81 (0)3-3428-8437
hassho.jp

The most famous Hiroshima-style *okonomiyaki* restaurant in Tokyo. The chef trained at the restaurant of the same name in Hiroshima and was given the green light to open this restaurant in Tokyo. Choose a seat at the counter where the chef will amaze you with his marvellous *okonomiyaki*-making technique.

87 MOMIJIYA
4-2-6 Iidabashi
Chiyoda-ku ⑨
+81 (0)3-6272-9320
momiji-ya.info

Another Hiroshima-style *okonomiyaki* restaurant. This place is so popular that there is almost always a queue outside. They serve *teppanyaki* and *yakisoba* (thin stir-fried noodles) or *yakiudon* (thick stir-fried noodles) as well as *okonomiyaki*.

88 HYOTAN
1-37-4 Asakusa
Taito-ku ⑩
+81 (0)3-3841-0589

Monjayaki, the soul food of *shitamachi* (downtown), is made with a more liquid batter than *okonomiyaki*. At monjayaki restaurants, a hot plate is incorporated into each table, and you are normally required to cook your dish yourself. If you are uncertain about how to do this, ask the staff – they are always helpful.

89 KAZAGURUMA JOSHUYA

3-16-4 Tsukishima
Chuo-ku ⑮
+81 (0)3-3534-5148

Although *monjayaki* is originally considered to be from Asakusa, Tsukishima is equally famous for it. Kazaguruma is one of the most popular places in the area with over 40 years of history. If you have never had *monjayaki* before, then try their *mentai mochi* (spicy cod roe and rice cake). You won't regret it.

90 SUZUME NO OYADO

9-3 Maruyamacho
Shibuya-ku ①
+81 (0)3-5458-2760
suzume-no-oyado.com

This area flourished as a post station during the Edo period, and became the entertainment and red-light district during the Meiji period. There are still many 'love hotels' here today but this restaurant used to be a *geisha* house. Their signature menu is Camembert Monja, a *monja* (batter) and a whole camembert cheese.

90 SUZUME NO OYADO

The 5 best places for other
ASIAN CUISINE

---

91 **ZUIEN BEKKAN**
2-7-4 Shinjuku
Shinjuku-ku ⑦
+81 (0)3-3351-3511
zuienbekkan.co.jp

An authentic Chinese restaurant on Shinjuku Street. *Bekkan* means 'annex' in Japanese, but there is no main building. You must taste their *sui gyoza* – its chewy texture is too good for words. Their *xiaolongbao* (steamed bun) is also highly recommended.

92 **FANSO**
2-12-10 Azabu Juban
Minato-ku ⑥
+81 (0)3-3456-6260
azabujubanfanso.web.
fc2.com

Many of Tokyo's Korean restaurants are located on Azabu Juban because of the nearby Korean Embassy. Fanso is said to be one of the best places for home-style dishes. Try their *gamjatang* (spicy pork bone stew) and *dak-galbi* (spicy stir-fried chicken).

93 **ANGKOR WAT**
1-38-13 Yoyogi
Shibuya-ku ⑦
+81 (0)3-3370-3019

A Cambodian restaurant, which opened in 1982. Their most popular dish is the stir-fried crab meat and vermicelli. The *kway teow*, served in a clear broth made from chicken bones, is also delicious. But the best thing on the menu must be their pumpkin cake, using real pumpkin skin, which is served with coconut ice cream.

94 AYUNG TERAS

20-12 Sakuragaokacho
Shibuya-ku ①
+81 (0)3-5458-9099
ayungteras.com

You may be forgiven for thinking you are in Bali in this authentic Indonesian restaurant. They even use Jenggala Keramik tableware. Most people order the *gado gado* (peanut sauce over boiled vegetables) and mixed satay. The deep-fried banana *pisang goreng* is also amazing.

95 THAILAND

3-12-10 Kinshi
Sumida-ku ⑮
+81 (0)3-3626-3885

The south exit of Kinshicho station is known as 'Little Thailand' and this restaurant is the oldest one in the area. They import all their ingredients from Thailand, so they serve real Thai food. Their *Thai suki* is very popular, and even those who traditionally shy away from spicy food love it in equal measure.

5 places you should go for
LATIN-AMERICAN CUISINE

96 **FONDA DE LA MADRUGADA**
2-33-12 Jingumae
Shibuya-ku ③
+81 (0)3-5410-6288
fonda-m.com

This restaurant opened in 1993 and soon became a place where people gather for a good time till dawn. They serve authentic Mexican cuisine and the music is performed by real *Mariachi*. As you go down the stairs to the basement, you might even forget that you are in Tokyo.

97 **GOSTOSO**
5-11-25 Roppongi
Minato-ku ⑥
+81 (0)3-6434-0243
gostoso.jp

This Brazilian restaurant is famous for its delicious char-grilled *churrasco*. In spring and summer, you can eat outside on the terrace. On weekends, they also serve lunch. As the restaurant's name suggests, their food is *gostoso* or delicious!

98 **TIA SUSANA**
8-11 Shinanomachi
Shinjuku-ku ⑦
+81 (0)3-3226-8511

This restaurant became a hit with the locals after it was featured in a popular manga series. While it is a Peruvian restaurant it is more like a sports bar – a football bar, to be precise. If you are looking for a place with a super atmosphere, where everyone loves football just as much as you do, then Tia Susana ticks all the boxes.

99 BÉPOCAH

2-17-6 Jingumae
Shibuya-ku ③
+81 (0)3-6804-1377
bepocah.com

Until a few years ago, Japanese people had never really tasted Peruvian cuisine. Taking advantage of the growing popularity of international travel and cuisine, a few restaurants opened in Harajuku, but Bépocah is the most sophisticated one. The chef, who is originally from Peru, uses ingredients from both Peru and Japan for his lovely fusion food. Don't forget to order some Pisco with your food!

100 BARBACOA

4-3-2 Jingumae
Shibuya-ku ③
+81 (0)3-3796-0571
barbacoa.jp

If you are a real meat lover, then this Brazilian restaurant is the equivalent of meat heaven. Their salad bar offers an amazing array of sides, that are all worth trying. They have several branches in Tokyo including in Shibuya and Roppongi.

5 places to grab a
ONE COIN (500 YEN) LUNCH

---

101 **KINTARO**
5-18-16 Shinjuku
Shinjuku-ku ⑦
+81 (0)3-5155-2917

Don't think you can eat *sukiyaki* (thinly-sliced beef cooked in sauce) for 500 yen? Well, this restaurant is proof to the contrary. Their *sukiyaki teishoku* (set meal) comes with a miso soup, salad, pickles, and a bowl of rice. Because of the quality and price, it is jam-packed during lunch hours.

102 **CONA**
15-17 Sakuragaokacho
Shibuya-ku ①
+81 (0)3-5459-5703
cona-sakura.com

A standing pizza bar serving thin crispy Rome-style pizzas at 500 yen. During lunch hours on weekdays, you can have pizza, salad, and drink at the same price. Just a short walk from Shibuya station. In the evening, they also serve pasta and other food.

103 **ICHIYOSHI**
1-4-1 Ebisu
Shibuya-ku ②
+81 (0)3-3444-0801

Ichiyoshi is an *izakaya* that offers a lunch menu at 500 yen (and 800 yen – still very reasonable!) at lunchtime. If you have a large appetite, then order one of their 'one-coin' menus (just 500 yen) called *mushidori no yakumi kake* (steamed chicken topped with relish and aromatic vegetables). No more hunger pangs for a while.

104 ALOHIDDIN

1-4-8 Hatchobori
Chuo-ku ⑧
+81 (0)3-6228-3898
alohiddin.web.fc2.com

The owner of this restaurant comes from Uzbekistan and serves Central Asian cuisine, which you can rarely find in Tokyo. *Kuru fasulye*, or stewed meat with white kidney beans, is a popular dish in Turkey and its neighbouring countries, and will set you back just 500 yen. The other lunch menus are all under 1000 yen.

105 DOGENZAKA ISARI

1-6-5 Dogenzaka
Shibuya-ku ⓪
+81 (0)3-6809-0991

Their signature *Isari Don* consists of a bowl of rice topped with sashimi, which is served with miso soup and pickles. The sashimi is marinated in a soy-based sauce, so you don't need to add any sauce although you can add a dash if you really feel you need it. The other lunch menus are slightly more expensive but still affordable.

5 restaurants
WHEN TIRED OF JAPANESE CUISINE

---

106 **PIGNON**
   16-3 Kamiyamacho
   Shibuya-ku ①
   +81 (0)3-3468-2331

An outstanding French bistro in Oku-Shibu (literally the 'back of Shibuya'). Where to start? Their salad with grilled squid on top, liver paté, homemade lamb sausage, … There are so many delectable things on the menu and their desserts are excellent too.

107 **HATAKE**
   5-7-2 Minami-Aoyama
   Minato-ku ③
   +81 (0)3-3498-0730
   hatake-aoyama.com

Hatake means a field where crops are grown. The chef of this Italian restaurant grows vegetables on the premises using natural farming methods. Enjoy some *bagna càuda* with a selection of these homegrown veggies. The terrine with seasonable vegetables is also worth trying.

108 **TA-IM**
   1-29-16 Ebisu
   Shibuya-ku ②
   +81 (0)3-5424-2990
   ta-imebisu.com

This is one of a handful of Israeli restaurants in Tokyo. It is located between Ebisu and Hiroo. They use neither preservatives nor frozen ingredients. Their hummus and falafel are very popular. Some of their dishes can be ordered as a takeaway. They serve pita bread sandwiches for lunchtime.

109 HANNIBAL

1-19-2 Hyakunincho
Shinjuku-ku ⑦
+81 (0)3-6304-0930
hannibal.jp

This restaurant, which opened in 1999, is the first Tunisian restaurant in Tokyo and is run by a Tunisian owner-chef. As you chat with the friendly and cheerful chef, you'll only become hungrier. The Tunisian *gyoza* (as the locals call it) or *brik* is simply delicious.

110 SUNGARI

AT: CHIYODA BUILDING
B1, 2-45-6 Kabukicho
Shinjuku-ku ⑦
+81 (0)3-3209-4937
sungari.jp

This Russian restaurant is an authentic Moscow-style restaurant and has been a popular fixture on the local scene for over fifty years. They serve a wide variety of dishes and vodkas. They have another branch in Shinjuku San-chome.

The 5 best
VEGETARIAN
restaurants

---

111 **8ABLISH**

2nd Fl., 5-10-17
Minami-Aoyama
Minato-ku ③
+81 (0)3-6805-0597
eightablish.com

The food and drink they serve here is all vegan, containing neither refined sugar nor food additives. If you eat gluten-free or have a sensitive stomach, this place might be a good option for you. The muffins and coffee are available for takeaway.

112 **EAT MORE GREENS**

2-2-5 Azabu Juban
Minato-ku ⑥
+81 (0)3-3798-3191
eatmoregreens.jp

This place opened in 2007, hoping to inspire people to eat more vegetables. Though they are not a vegetarian restaurant per se, they have plenty of menu options for vegetarians and vegans. The beverage menu includes smoothies, homemade ginger ale, and organic coffee made from freshly-ground beans.

113 **BROWN RICE**
BY NEAL'S YARD REMEDIES

5-1-8 Jingumae
Shibuya-ku ③
+81 (0)3-5778-5416
nealsyard.co.jp

An organic vegetarian restaurant run by UK-based Neal's Yard Remedies. Their set lunch consists of one soup and three different dishes, including pickles. They also have vegetable and bean curry. Their desserts, which are all tofu-based, such as cheesecake and ice cream, are delicious.

114 THREE AOYAMA REVIVE KITCHEN

3-12-13 Kita-Aoyama Minato-ku ③
+81 (0)3-6419-7513
aoyama.threecosmetics. com

The restaurant section of cosmetic brand Three. They are open from 8 am till 10 pm. Their breakfast will boost your energy and they have plenty of gluten-free options as well. If you are the type who believes in healthy and balanced nutrition, then you'll be happy to know they have cold-pressed juices too.

115 NTARAJ

AT: SANWA-AOYAMA BUILDING
2-22-19 Minami-Aoyama Minato-ku ④
+81 (0)3-5474-0510
nataraj2.sakura.ne.jp

The first vegetarian Indian restaurant in Japan. The chef mixes all the spices and they use no food additives. What's more, they own three farms where they grow their own organic vegetables. Some of their dishes are also suited for macrobiotic eaters.

5 nice restaurants
WITH A VIEW

---

116 TWO ROOMS GRILL / BAR
AT: AO BUILDING, 5TH FL.
3-11-7 Kita-Aoyama
Minato-ku ③
+81 (0)3-3498-0002
tworooms.jp

This restaurant is located on the fifth floor of a landmark tower in Omotesando. From their terrace, you can enjoy a typical view of Tokyo's cityscape – lots of skyscrapers, but it all feels amazingly open and relaxing. This place doesn't just have a good view, they also serve excellent food. A kids menu is available for the under-12 crowd.

117 HANA CHIBO
AT: EBISU GARDEN PLACE TOWER, 38TH FL.
4-20-3 Ebisu
Shibuya-ku ②
+81 (0)3-5424-1011
chibo.com

This place is run by Osaka's *okonomiyaki* chain. Here, you don't have to cook your own *okonomiyaki* – their chefs make it for you. There are two counters (and tables), one where you can take in the view and another where you can enjoy the spectacle of the chef's cooking techniques.

118 MOCHIZUKI
AT: ASAHI GOUP HQ BUILDING, 21ST FL.
1-23-11 Azumabashi
Sumida-ku ⑮
+81 (0)3-5608-5002

A Japanese restaurant located on the 21st floor of the Asahi Beer Company's headquarters which is probably famous for the golden object designed by Philip Stark. From the restaurant, you can enjoy a panoramic view of the Tokyo Skytree and the Sumida River.

119 STELLER GARDEN

AT: THE PRINCE PARK TOWER
TOKYO, 33RD FL.
**4-8-1 Shibakoen
Minato-ku ⑥
+81 (0)3-5400-1154**
princehotels.com

The bar lounge in the Prince Park Tower Tokyo, a hotel located near the Tokyo Tower. Their signature menu is their Kobe beef hamburger. A bit expensive overall because of the location, but if you want to spend a romantic evening with the love of your life, this can be a great choice.

120 VIEW AND DINING THE SKY

AT: HOTEL NEW OTANI,
17TH FL.
**4-1 Kioicho
Chiyoda-ku ⑤
+81 (0)3-3238-0028**
newotani.co.jp

This buffet-style restaurant slowly rotates 360 degrees. Try Japanese, Western or Chinese food, *teppanyaki*, and sushi as well as the desserts. The sushi here is still made to order. They serve top-class Japanese beef steak in the *teppanyaki* corner.

APÉRO. WINEBAR & TABLE

55 PLACES
FOR A DRINK

5 Japanese
ALCOHOLIC BEVERAGES

─────

121 **SAKE**

Sake, also referred to as Japanese rice wine, is made by fermenting rice. There are eight varieties of special designation sake, distinguished by the degree to which the rice has been polished and the percentage of malt, and whether brewing alcohol is added or not. *Junmai Daiginjo* is the highest quality. If you like sake, you should also try milky-coloured *Nigori-zake*, which is produced by straining sake through rough gauze.

122 **CHUHAI**

An abbreviation for 'shochu highball'. Ordinarily a mix of *shochu*, soda, and fruit juice, mainly citrus. It is also called '*sour*' because of its taste. At some *izakaya* (Japanese-style pubs), *chuhai* is served with half a lemon or grapefruit on a press.

123 **UMESHU**

Widely known as 'plum wine'. In Japan, many people produce their own *umeshu* at home. It is not difficult to make: just steep green plums in a distilled alcoholic beverage, such as *shochu*, brandy, or white liquor. Drink it like you would drink *shochu*, but it is also delicious when mixed with beer.

124 AWAMORI

This distilled alcoholic beverage is made of rice produced in Okinawa Prefecture. *Awamori* uses Indica rice (long grain) while *shochu* uses Japonica rice (short grain). The type of mould used is also different. Like *shochu*, you can drink it on the rocks, diluted with water, hot water, or soda. Add a dash of *shekwasha* (flat lemon), if you like your *awamori* old school.

125 SHOCHU

Distilled liquor made from wheat, buckwheat, rice, or sweet potatoes. *Kokuto* (unpurified sugar) *shochu* is produced on Amami Island and Okinawa, where sugar cane grows. If you are lucky, you may also come across other varieties of *shochu*, including chestnut, sweet corn, milk, and pumpkin.

121 SAKE

5
ESSENTIAL BEVERAGES
that you can buy in a convenience store

---

126 I-LOHAS

The name is pronounced as 'Irohasu' and refers to natural water in PET bottles. In addition to still water, you can also buy fruit-flavoured waters, such as *mikan* (clementine) and apple, and sparkling water. They support 'lifestyles of health and sustainability' (LOHAS, for short). The bottles are easy to squash, reducing waste.

127 MITSUYA SAIDA

This carbonated drink was developed in 1884 using Japanese mineral water. It owes its flavour to fresh fruit harvested in the past 24 hours. These products do not contain preservatives. Some drinks are available in a low-calorie version.

128 POCARI SWEAT

A healthy drink that helps your body absorb water quickly, making it an ideal sports drink. Many Japanese people drink it when they have a fever, and doctors often recommend it for this purpose. It is also a good drink for a summer hike or if you had too much alcohol.

129 **AYATAKA**

A type of Japanese green tea, packaged in PET bottles and developed in collaboration with a tea shop in Uji (where *Uji-cha* is produced) that has been in business for over 450 years. It tastes so good that you might not even notice the difference with tea brewed in a teapot. From mild to full-bodied, there is one for everyone. Hot tea is also available.

130 **CALPIS**

A lactobacillus beverage that has been a favourite with Japanese people for over a century. Originally a concentrated beverage to be diluted with water, it was inspired by a drink from Inner Mongolia. Nowadays it is also sold in PET bottles. Choose from fruit-flavoured, carbonated, low-calorie and several other options.

The 5 best places for
SAKE

---

131 **FUKUBE**
1-4-5 Yaesu
Chuo-ku ⑧
+81 (0)3-3271-6065

While this *izakaya* (Japanese-style pub) has been in business for over 80 years, their selection of sake hasn't changed much since the early days. In Japan, people eat while they drink so bar food is just as important as quality of the drinks you are served. The owner of this bar goes to Tsukiji market every day to buy the catch of the day.

132 **HASEGAWA**
AT: OMOTESANDO HILLS,
3RD FL.
4-12-10 Jingumae
Shibuya-ku ③
+81 (0)3-5785-0833
hasegawasaketen.com

The owners of this liquor shop are considered fine connoisseurs of the sake industry and have the best selection of sake in Tokyo. They also serve sake in a shot glass at the counter as well as snacks that pair very nicely with your drink. If you want to taste a line-up of different brands, then this is the place to go.

133 **KAWAGUCHI**
2-9-6 Nihonbashi
Chuo-ku ⑧
+81 (0)3-6225-2850

A standing sake bar. The manager used to be a sushi chef, so he has his own policy when it comes to fish – he does not use farmed fish and thinks about how best to serve fish so that it pairs nicely with your drink.

134 **KURI**
AT: TONY BUILDING, 2ND FL.
6-4-15 Ginza
Chuo-ku ⑧
+81 (0)3-3573-8033

A small bar in Ginza that serves 50 to 100 brands of sake and 20 brands of shochu. If you can't find a brand you like here, you won't find it anywhere else. When the bar is busy, they may not be able to take phone enquiries, so make sure you have Google Maps on your phone.

135 **UTOU**
3-31-10 Nishiogi-Kita
Suginami-ku
+81 (0)3-3399-1890

Nishi-Ogikubo, often called 'Nishi Ogi', is very popular with intellectuals and antiques lovers. As this shop is said to serve the best warm sake in all of Japan, you can usually find loads of sake enthusiasts here. The *oden* they serve, with a ginger and miso paste, is simply excellent.

131 FUKUBE

5 must-visit
BARS IN SHINJUKU GOLDEN-GAI

---

136 AKAHANA
1-1-8 Kabukicho
Shinjuku-ku ⑦

This bar serves a good selection of *awamori* (Okinawa's shochu) and Okinawan cuisine. You can drink *awamori* diluted with turmeric tea or *sanpin-cha* (jasmine tea) just like in Okinawa. It is always crowded with regulars who love the friendly owner's home cooking.

137 ISHI NO HANA
1-1-10 Kabukicho
Shinjuku-ku ⑦
+81 (0)3-3200-8458

A small Russian *izakaya* that opened in 1973, making it one of the oldest in the area. The owner will gladly get out his guitar when asked. Do try their selection of vodkas if you go – some of them are quite rare.

138 BIG RIVER
1-1-6 Kabukicho
Shinjuku-ku ⑦
+81 (0)3-3209-6418

Traditionally, Golden-gai is popular with people who work in the publishing industry, especially editors. The owner of this bar used to be an editor, so editors, manga artists and designers all gather at this bar. People normally go on a 'bar stroll' in the area. This is the place to go when you feel peckish. The beef rice curry is a favourite on the menu.

139 BAR URAMEN

1-1-7 Kabukicho
Shinjuku-ku ⑦
+81 (0)80-4369-9713
971.jp

A themed *otaku* bar: home electrical appliances and digital gadgets as well as retro games. Enjoy drinks and games here, as they have roughly 600 FamiCon cassettes, while listening to some weirdly cool music.

140 TACHIBANA SHINSATSUSHITSU

1-1-8 Kabukicho
Shinjuku-ku ⑦
+81 (0)3-3208-4148

This bar's concept is that of a waiting room at a hospital. The staff wear nurse uniforms. All the cocktails have unique names. If you do not understand Japanese, ask the *nurse*. But be warned, some of the names are rather outrageous. Don't be disgusted, it is just their unique sense of humour.

136-140 GOLDEN-GAI

140 TACHIBANA SHINSATSUSHITSU

The 5 best places for
JAPANESE CRAFT BEER

141 **T.Y. HARBOR**
2-1-3 Higashi-Shinagawa
Shinagawa-ku ⑭
+81 (0)3-5479-4555
tysons.jp

This place started out as brewery restaurant in 1997, three years after the ban on producing craft beers was lifted, renovating part of a warehouse. Beer is an ingredient in some of the dishes on the menu, including grilled ale-marinated chicken and mussels steamed in ale.

142 **INAZUMA DINING**
3-6-9 Roppongi
Minato-ku ⑥
+81 (0)3-6441-2802

Inazuma Beer is a brewery in a residential area in the centre of Tokyo. Their craft beers are served at Inazuma Dining, a bar at the same address where you can also eat. They serve excellent food, made with seasonal organic vegetables that pair nicely with their beer.

143 **NIHONBASHI BREWERY**
AT: &WORK NIHONBASHI,
1ST FL.
10-13 Nihonbashi
Tomizawacho
Chuo-ku ⑨
+81 (0)3-6231-0226

You can enjoy 15 brands of craft beer including the original one specially created by Oregon's HUB (Hop works Urban Brewery). They use pesticide-free or low pesticide ingredients for the food menu. There is another shop near Tokyo station.

144 SHUJITSU ONE

3-44-11 Uehara
Shibuya-ku ⑫
+81 (0)3-5738-8501
shujitsu.com/one

A good place for craft beers and organic wine. Their main brand is Minoo Beer, a popular brand produced in Minoo City, Osaka. Try it with chicken and chips with a tasty tartar sauce. They share the floor with an Ethiopian coffee shop called TO.MO.CA.

145 CRAFT BEER MARKET

AT: SUMITOMO SHOJI
JINBOCHO BUILDING, 1ST FL.
2-11-15 Kanda Jinbocho
Chiyoda-ku ⑨
+81 (0)3-6272-5652
craftbeermarket.jp

They sell about 30 different craft beers here including Japanese and import brands. If you don't want to stop at one, then perhaps you should consider the *nomi hodai* option (drink all you can). Their signature food is roast chicken.

145 CRAFT BEER MARKET

5 great
WINE BARS

---

146 **AOI**
2nd Fl.
1-18-9 Sekiguchi
Bunkyo-ku ⑩
+81 (0)3-6823-8246
winebar-aoi.com

This wine bar serves a selection of Japanese wines as well as French, Italian, California, and other import wines. They serve a selection of cheeses chosen by an affineur and snacks made from Japanese ingredients that go well with wines. They occasionally organise tastings.

147 **BAR À VIN PARTAGER**
AT: OMOTESANDO HILLS,
3RD FL.
4-12-10 Jingumae
Shibuya-ku ③
+81 (0)3-6434-9091
partager-omotesando.com

A wine bar in Omotesando Hills that serves wine from Japan, Europe and South America, and champagne at reasonable prices. Half a glass of wine will set you back just under 300 yen! They also serve their casual take on top-notch French cuisine. Do order their foie gras macaron.

148 **3AMOURS**
1-15-9 Ebisu-Nishi
Shibuya-ku ②
+81 (0)3-5459-4333
3amours.com

A wine bar in a wine shop. You can enjoy a glass (or glasses) of organic wine at a reasonable price – even if you are on your own. A nice wine shop where you may discover some interesting and rare finds. Bear in mind they close at 9 pm.

149 **SHIZUKU**

**3-6-47 Kagurazaka
Shinjuku-ku** ⑦
+81 (0)3-6265-3790
kagurazakashizuku.com

This wine bar is located in an 80-year-old house in a back street in Kagurazaka. Here they serve Italian cuisine made with outstanding Japanese ingredients that pair nicely with the wines on their menu. They have a second-floor room for groups of 8 to 16 people with a two-hour *nomi hodai* option (drink all you can).

150 **APÉRO. WINE BAR & TABLE**

**3-4-6 Minami-Aoyama
Minato-ku** ④
+81 (0)3-6325-3893
apero.co.jp

A wine bar run by a French couple serving organic, biodynamic, or natural wines imported from wineries that were personally selected by the owner. They serve French cuisine made with organic Japanese ingredients and organise fun-filled events.

150 APÉRO. WINE BAR & TABLE

The 5 best places for
JAPANESE TEA

---

151 CHA CHA NO MA
5-13-14 Jingumae
Shibuya-ku ③
+81 (0)3-5468-8846
chachanoma.com

Tea sommelier Yoshi Watada serves a selection of teas from all over Japan. The food menu, including homemade sweets, is excellent and their *matcha* (green tea) ice cream comes highly recommended. Don't forget to order *kiseki no itteki* (which is a surprise drink).

152 UOGASHI MEICHA
5-5-6 Ginza
Chuo-ku ⑧
+81 (0)3-3571-1211
uogashi-meicha.co.jp

Their main shop is located right in the heart of Tsukiji Market and has been popular with people in Tokyo for many years. Their Ginza shop is the place to go for a nice cup of tea with a slice of seasonal Japanese cake. Their light-coloured *hoji-cha* (roasted tea) is very mild.

153 KOSOAN
1-24-23 Jiyugaoka
Meguro-ku ⑬
+81 (0)3-3718-4203
kosoan.co.jp

A cafe in an old traditional house that was built over a century ago. You might be forgiven for thinking that you escaped busy Tokyo as you gaze at their lovely Japanese garden. Enjoy your bowl of *matcha* in this soothing atmosphere. Their antique furniture is also worth looking at.

154 **CHA-NO-HA**
AT: MATSUYA GINZA
3-6-1 Ginza
Chuo-ku ⑧
+81 (0)3-3567-2635
chanoha.info

Located in the basement of Matsuya, behind the retail space. You can enjoy tea and seasonal sweets at the counter. This place is a real life-saver when you need a break from shopping in Ginza. The menu is seasonal.

155 **CHA CHA KOBO**
2-21-19 Nishi-Waseda
Shinjuku-ku ⑪
+81 (0)3-3203-2033
chachakoubou.com

This cafe serves organic Japanese tea and Japanese sweets, including *matcha* ice cream and *zenzai* (*mochi* and sweet red bean sauce). They also have rice balls at lunch, and *udon* noodles and bowl food in the evening.

153 **KOSOAN**

The 5 cosiest
COFFEE SHOPS

156 **MANMANDO**
3-15-4 Nishi-Nippori
Arakawa-ku ⑩
+81 (0)3-3824-4800

This cafe has a unique atmosphere, with antique furniture and the pleasing aroma of homeroasted beans. The owner does not believe in compromises when it comes to beans. Some of the beans they roast here are so rare that you should give them a try.

157 **GRAMERCY COFFEE BAR**
3-7-2 Minami-Aoyama
Minato-ku ④
+81 (0)3-6432-9874
gramercycoffee.jp
(only Japanese)

Located on a street off route 246, this cafe has a friendly atmosphere. They serve homeroasted coffee and delicious homemade cakes and cookies. Almond milk is available as a vegetarian and dairy- or soy-free option.

158 **KANDA COFFEE**
2-38-10 Kanda Jinbocho
Chiyoda-ku ⑨
+81 (0)3-5213-4337

A coffee house located in an area with plenty of bookshops. A pretty red roaster welcomes you when you get tired of book-hunting. Many business people like to come here for a coffee on their lunch break.

159 SANJIKKEN

3-8-12 Ginza
Chuo-ku ⑧
+81 (0)3-3564-8096
yanaka-coffeeten.com

A cafe run by the Tokyo-based coffee bean merchant Yanaka Coffee, which has over 30 shops in Tokyo. Here coffee comes in a coffee server so customers can enjoy a refill. They have another cafe in Omotesando.

160 JALK COFFEE

4-19-4 Eifuku
Suginami-ku ⑫
+81 (0)3-6379-1313
jalkcoffee.com

Their concept is 'to offer people a bit of happiness with coffee in their daily life'. Good news for coffee addicts: the second cup is half-price. Do try their homemade chiffon cake.

158 KANDA COFFEE

5
SHOWA-STYLE CAFES

---

161 **COFFEE L'AMBRE**
3-31-3 Shinjuku
Shinjuku-ku ⑦
+81 (0)3-3352-3361

A boring characterless cafe at first glance, but walk downstairs and it's like travelling back in time to the Showa period (1926-1989). As they are open till late, this is a good option for an after-dinner coffee.

162 **MILONGA NUEVA**
1-3 Kanda Jinbocho
Chiyoda-ku ⑨
+81 (0)3-3295-1716

There are several old cafes in Jinbocho, and this perhaps is one of the most famous ones. As the name suggests, this is a tango cafe where live tango concerts are sometimes held. Try their pear tart or chocolate pudding, which both taste equally well with coffee. They also serve beer.

163 **LADRIO**
1-3 Kanda Jinbocho
Chiyoda-ku ⑨
+81 (0)3-3295-4788

This cafe, which is located in the same alley as Milonga, resonates with French chansons. They are the first cafe to serve Wiener coffee. Wax nostalgic as you listen to the distinctive sound of vinyl records in dimmed light over a coffee.

164 MEIKYOKU KISSA LION

2-19-13 Dogenzaka
Shibuya-ku ①
+81 (0)3-3461-6858
lion.main.jp

A *meikyoku kissa* is a type of cafe where customers can enjoy classical music (often played on an expensive audio system) while enjoying coffee or tea. This cafe opened in 1926. It was burnt down during WWII but subsequently reopened. Please note that taking pictures and using a mobile phone is not allowed here.

165 CAFÉ PAULISTA

8-9-16 Ginza
Chuo-ku ⑮
+81 (0)3-3572-6160
paulista.co.jp

The term *Ginbura*, which means drinking Brazilian coffee in Ginza, was coined by the regulars of this cafe. Café Paulista opened in 1911 and is popular with a great many people including the legendary John Lennon. The coffee beans they use are certified organic.

161 COFFEE L'AMBRE

The 5 most interesting
ANIMAL CAFES

---

166 **MIAGOLARE**
AT: DAINI FUJIO BUILDING,
3RD FL.
4-30-26 Honcho
Nakano-ku ⑫
+81 (0)3-6382-8105
miagolare.org

You pay the entrance fee, enjoy drinks and get to play with cats. All the cats were rescued from getting killed. This cafe is a place where rescued cats and people wishing to adopt one can meet. But the cats are equally happy with visitors who just want to pet them.

167 **MUGIMARU 2**
5-20 Kagurazaka
Shinjuku-ku ⑤
+81 (0)3-5228-6393
mugimaru2.com

This cafe in an old house serves a variety of buns. As it happens, they also have cats that wander about freely. Their upstairs feels very much like home. On hot days there may not be a cat in sight. Where are they, you wonder? Who knows? They are cats after all.

168 **IKEFUKURO**
AT: SAKIMOTO BUILDING,
6TH FL.
1-17-1 Minami-Ikebukuro
Toshima-ku ⑪
+81 (0)3-3988-2914
ikefukuroucafe.com

They have about 50 owls in this cafe. Owl, *fukuro* in Japanese, rhymes with Ikebukuro, so the owl is the symbol of this area. You can bring your own owl (quite a few people own owls as pets in Japan) if you wish but you must inform cafe staff before your visit. Please note they only serve drinks in PET bottles, no food.

169 FOREST OF OWL

4-5-8 Sotokanda
Chiyoda-ku ⑨
+81 (0)3-3254-6366
2960.tokyo

This is Tokyo's largest owl cafe although it doesn't look like a cafe, really. As its name suggests, this place resembles a forest, and you might have difficulty in discovering an owl at first. Some of the owls are used to humans, others are not. Be careful not to touch the wild ones.

170 HACHURUI KUKAN

AT: FUJI DAINI BUILDING,
3RD FL.
5-10-1 Arai
Nakano-ku ⑫
+81 (0)3-5318-9357

Hachurui means reptiles. Yes, this is a cafe where you can play with reptiles. This cafe is members only. Ring them up the day before your visit. They also offer a hotel for reptiles, so, they can look after your pets for you while you are out of town.

168 IKEFUKURO

5 great places for
COLD-PRESSED JUICES

---

171 **ELLE CAFE**
5-51-8 Jingumae
Shibuya-ku ③
+81 (0)3-6451-1996
ellecafe.jp

A popular place, not just with health-conscious youngsters but with all young people. On weekends, there is always a long queue around the lunch hour, but they are open from 8 am (9 am on weekdays) so why not have breakfast there? A great place to try some *coyo* (coconut yoghurt). They have gluten-free options too.

172 **DAVID OTTO**
2-6-3 Sendagaya
Shibuya-ku ③
+81 (0)3-6758-0620
davidottojuice.com

A Tokyo branch of a Californian cold-pressed juice shop. Their coconut water is sourced from old coconut, so its texture is thicker than the water of young coconuts. You can add a scoop of coconut ice cream from Kippy's Coco Cream which share this shop space with David Otto.

173 **CLEANSING CAFE**
22-12 Sarugakucho
Shibuya-ku ②
+81 (0)3-6277-5336
cleansingcafe.com

In addition to a variety of cold pressed juices, including seasonal ones, they also serve soup as a detox option. They recommend having some wild rice with it. You can take away juice and soup. They can also put together a diet menu for you.

174 SUNSHINE JUICE

1-5-8 Ebisu
Shibuya-ku ②
+81 (0)3-6277-3122
sunshinejuice.jp

The pioneer of cold-pressed juice in Japan. They use locally-sourced ingredients as much as possible. They even visit farmers to see how fruit and vegetables are grown and buy ugly fruit and vegetables that won't make it to market. As you can see, their juice makes everyone happy. Smoothies and vegan soups also available.

175 TRUEBERRY

5-4-18 Hiroo
Shibuya-ku ②
+81 (0)3-6450-3952
trueberry.jp

Here they only use organic ingredients that were produced in Japan, so if you care about food miles, then this is the perfect place for you. In addition to cold-pressed juice, they also serve a range of smoothies and raw cakes that will satisfy any sweet tooth.

100 PLACES TO SHOP

———————

5
FASHION *shops for* **MEN**

---

176 **BEAMS**
3-24-7 Jingumae
Shibuya-ku ③
+81 (0)3-3470-3947
beams.co.jp

Beams is one of the pioneering select shops and opened in the seventies. They stock casual clothes by Japanese and import brands. As this is an essential shop for Harajuku fashion, there are several Beams shops, including Beams T, which sells graphic T-shirts, and a shop for women, called Beams Boy, in the same area, with clothes that are inspired by men's fashion.

177 **MASTERMIND**
AT: TOKYO MIDTOWN HIBIYA
2-5-1 Yurakucho
Chiyoda-ku ⑧
mastermindjapan.com

For fashionistas who visit Tokyo, Mastermind is one of the must-go places. This is a new outlet. The brand's flagship store opened in March 2018. Casual but chic. Wild but stylish. Perhaps you should add one of their items to your wardrobe?

178 **NIKELAB MA5**
5-12-24 Minami-Aoyama
Minato-ku ③
+81 (0)3-6427-2560
nike.com/jp/ja_jp/c/
nikelab/ma5

A Nike shop that sells trainers and clothes for both men and women is located in the former private swimming pool for the residents of the building. Men's trainers are available from 24 cm (or size 5,5 UK), so they can be worn by women!

179 KURA CHIKA YOSHIDA

5-6-8 Jingumae
Shibuya-ku ③
+81 (0)3-5464-1766
yoshidakaban.com

Yoshida Kaban, of the Porter and Luggage Label brands, has been producing quality leather goods since 1935. Their range includes business and casual and everything in between. They also have a line of bags for women. Their products are all equally practical and stylish.

180 STUDIOUS

4-26-32 Jingumae
Shibuya-ku ③
+81 (0)3-5785-1864
studious-onlinestore.com

This select shop sells only clothes by Tokyo brands, which includes internationally-renowned brands such as Miyahara Yasuhiro and Undercover. They also stock clothes by emerging designers who may rise to global fame in the future. You never know!

5
FASHION shops for WOMEN

181 **MINÄ PERHONEN**
AT: HILLSIDE TERRACE G,
1ST FL.
18-12 Sarugakucho
Shibuya-ku ②
+81 (0)3-6826-3770
mina-perhonen.jp

The textile designer Akira Minagawa's brand has been a wardrobe staple for several generations of women. Minagawa's creations combine loads of different elements, from elegant to *kawaii*. Sometimes the designer is in the shop so have a chat with him if you happen to run into him.

182 **TSUMORI CHISATO**
4-21-25 Minami-Aoyama
Minato-ku ④
+81 (0)3-3423-5170
tsumorichisato.cc

Chisato Tsumori has been producing her range of cute and happy clothes since the eighties. You may think it's all too pretty for you, but give one of her designs a whirl and you might have a change of heart. She designs with mature women in mind, not for girls.

183 **HYKE**
AT: ISETAN RE-STYLE
3-14-1 Shinjuku
Shinjuku-ku ⑦
+81 (0)3-3352-1111
hyke.jp

A Japanese brand that attracts attention from all over the world. It was launched in 2013 by two Japanese designers who had already worked in the fashion industry. They use primary colours, such as khaki and black, and while their designs are simple, they are never boring.

184 SIMMON

18-5 Uguisudani
Shibuya-ku ①
+81 (0)3-6455-3467
simmon-s.com

The atelier and shop of the young Japanese jewellery designer Shimon Sato, whose works are sold in shops in and outside of Japan, including at the MoMA. He creates works with tiny animal motifs, including wolf and deer, which are totally cute. Drop him an e-mail first to see whether he is in.

185 JURGEN LEHL + BABAGHURI

AT: SHIN KOKUSAI BUILDING, 1ST FL.
3-4-1 Marunouchi
Chiyoda-ku ⑧
+81 (0)3-6212-0082
jurgenlehl.jp

The late German-born Japan-based designer Jurgen Lehl created a timeless style with flowing clothes, in comfy fabrics, that can be worn for years. The scarves work well in every season and the accessories are beautiful in a very simple way.

184 SIMMON

5 places where you can buy
'THE ONLY ONE
IN THE WORLD'

---

186 PIECE
3-41-3 Jingumae
Shibuya-ku ③
+81 (0)3-6440-0163
mina-perhonen.jp

Minä Perhonen's 'Upcycle' shop. The accessories here are made of odds and ends, scraps of textiles and remade items from Minä's archive collection. The items are displayed in beautiful antique furniture. You may find yourself browsing for longer than you intended as you try to pick the right brooch for you. And why not, there are so many options to choose from.

187 KEISUKE KANDA
AT: HOKUTO DAIICHI BUILDING,
3RD FL.
2-14-3 Yoyogi
Shibuya-ku ⑦
+81 (0)3-6276-2995
keisukekanda.com

A young Japanese designer who expresses his unique take on the world with his own clothes collection. At first glance his designs may look very basic and simple but Keisuke Kanda is very particular about stitches and how he puts together clothes, which shows why they are quite different. The tiny elephant logo looks very cute.

188 WHITE ATELIER
BY CONVERSE
6-16-5 Jingumae
Shibuya-ku ③
+81 (0)3-5778-4170
whiteatelier-by-converse.jp

In the basement of this shop, there is a workshop where you can buy a pair of completely white Chuck Taylors. Then you choose your illustration and add studs or charms for your own custom design.

189 DESERTIC

2-26-7 Nishi-Azabu
Minato-ku ④
+81 (0)3-6427-5156
desertic-tokyo.com

A Japanese unisex casual brand designed by Takeaki Taira. Its signature 'liquid' series features a liquid-shaped patchwork made from a vintage T-shirt, knit, or scarf on a plain white shirt. Each item is unique. Shirts with hand-painted borders, mountain parkas, and accessories are also available.

190 SUPER A MARKET

3-18-9 Minami-Aoyama
Minato-ku ④
+81 (0)3-3423-8428
superamarket.jp

A select shop stocking everything from designs by talented young Japanese designers to international luxury brands. Handmade accessories made by the Tokyo-based French bead designer Armel Malejacq are definitely worth checking out. He usually is in the shop a few days a week to customise the clothes.

189 DESERTIC

5
DESIGNER CLOTHES
shops

---

191 FACETASM

2-31-9 Jingumae
Shibuya-ku ③
+81 (0)3-6447-2852
facetasm.jp

The designer Hiromichi Ochiai established this brand in 2007. His creations soon caught the eye of the fashion-conscious crowd. Every item he designs has a distinctive shape, sometimes he adds cute frills. May not work as a head to toe look for you, but perhaps one item may be a good addition to your wardrobe?

192 SACAI

5-4-44 Minami-Aoyama
Minato-ku ④
+81 (0)3-6418-5977
sacai.jp

Sacai was established by the Japanese designer Chitose Abe in 1999. Since then it has become one of the world's leading fashion brands. Abe's creations are a good mix of sweet and sharp, or cute and cool.

193 UNDERCOVER

5-3-22 Minami-Aoyama
Minato-ku ④
+81 (0)3-3407-1232
undercoverism.com

The Japanese designer Jun Takahashi established this brand while he was still in fashion college. As he only produced limited editions of his clothes, Undercover soon had a cult following. The collaboration with Nike Gyakusou is very popular with fashion-conscious runners.

194 DOVER STREET MARKET GINZA

6-9-5 Ginza
Chuo-ku ⑧
+81 (0)3-6228-5080
ginza.doverstreet
market.com

Dover Street Market is a fashion department store run by Comme des Garçons, and this is their Ginza outlet. As well as CdG's brands, including Junya Watanabe and Noir Kei Ninomiya, they also stock many renowned brands, such as Balenciaga and Louis Vuitton. Pop over to the Rose Bakery on the seventh floor for some cake to give your feet a rest after all the shopping.

195 HYSTERIC GLAMOUR

6-23-2 Jingumae
Shibuya-ku ③
Women:
+81 (0)3-3409-7227
Men:
+81 (0)3-3797-5910
hystericglamour.jp

This brand was established in the eighties and was inspired by the American culture and fashion scene from the sixties to the eighties. The clothes are colourful and full of rock 'n' roll flair and will make you feel empowered. They also carry a kids' collection.

5 not-to-miss
VINTAGE shops

196 **EVA**
Avenue side
Daikanyama1B
2-1 Sarugakucho
Shibuya-ku ①
+81 (0)3-5489-2488
evavintagetokyo.com

The owner believes vintage clothes play a vital part in today's fashion industry. In fact, fashionable people like to mix vintage items with clothes from high fashion brands. The items EVA sells are all in mint condition and will look good in any wardrobe.

197 **TOGA XTC**
6-31-10 Jingumae
Shibuya-ku ③
+81 (0)3-6419-8136
toga.jp/store

The vintage clothes shop of the Japanese brand Toga's designer Yasuko Furuta. Located in the parking lot of Toga's Harajuku shop. This small shop stocks plenty of dresses, bags, shoes, and accessories from the seventies and eighties.

198 **VELVET**
AT: SUZURAN BUILDING,
1ST FL.
3-26-3 Kitazawa
Setagaya-ku ⑫
+81 (0)3-6407-8770
velvet.pw

The owner used to work as an editor. Although he had no previous experience as a clothes buyer or a shop owner, he has always worn vintage clothes. So he selects items from a (former) editor's point of view. Mainly for men, but women can also wear the stuff he sells if they like an oversized look.

199 **PASS THE BATON**
AT: MARUNOUCHI BRICK
SQUARE

2-6-1 Marunouchi
Chiyoda-ku ⑧
+81 (0)3-6269-9555
pass-the-baton.com

These clothes and accessories are passed to future users, much like a baton is passed on to the next runner. Many of the preloved items on sale here were previously owned by people in the fashion industry, such as stylists. Their eco bags – made by printing their original illustration on dead stock eco bags - are an excellent example of 'upcycling'.

200 **LEMONTEA**

6-11-8 Jingumae
Shibuya-ku ③
+81 (0)3-5467-2407
blog.lemontea-tokyo.net

From Nike vintage trainers to Harris Tweed jackets, they stock a variety of basic standard items from the United States and Europe. Vintage outdoor clothes that are wearable in the city and look cool. All items mix and match nicely with your non-vintage items.

199. PASS THE BATON

5 *great places to*
BUY A KIMONO

---

201 OYAMA KIMONO C'ERA UNA VOLTA

3-14-9 Minami-Aoyama
Minato-ku ④
+81 (0)3-3479-8045
oyamakimono.com

Located on a back street in Aoyama, they sell good quality antique kimonos. They also offer kimono-wearing lessons if you decide to buy one for yourself. Or you can ask them to help dress you. They also sell original *obi* (belts) made from import fabrics.

202 OEDO KAZUKO

4-29-3 Jingumae
Shibuya-ku ③
+81 (0)3-5785-1045
ooedokazuko.
ooedo-group.com

This shop is run by an antiques and art dealer, so they have an eye when it comes to buying kimonos in mint condition. They stock several *furisode* (with long sleeves, worn by young unmarried women) as well as men's kimonos. They also have the right hair accessories for when you wear a kimono.

203 SETAGAYA BORO ICHI

Setagaya
Setagaya-ku

The ultimate place to buy kimonos. Setagaya Boro Ichi is a flea market that has been held in December and January of every year since 1578. *Boro* means 'worn-out' and *ichi* is an abbreviation of *ichiba* (market). Who knows, you may even be able to score some bargains here.

204 TOKYO HOTARUDO

1-41-8 Asakusa
Taito-ku ⑩
+81 (0)3-3845-7563
tokyohotarudo.com

The place to go for vintage clothes. They have many items of the Taisho period (1912-1926). The kimonos of that era are quite colourful and fashionable and you can wear boots with them. They have accessories to go with the kimono.

205 OLD & NEW TANSUYA

AT: NAKAYAMA BUILDING,
1ST FL.

3-4-5 Ginza
Chuo-ku ⑧
+81 (0)3-3561-8529
tansuya.jp

Tansuya is a used kimono shop. At their Ginza shop, you can buy kimonos for formal occasions. Try this shop if you are serious about purchasing a quality kimono (and are not on a budget).

5 must-visit
CONCEPT STORES

---

206 MAISON DE MARUYAMA

4-25-10 Minami-Aoyama
Minato-ku ④
+81 (0)3-3406-1935
keitamaruyama.com

The concept store of fashion designer Keita Maruyama where he creates something exciting and impressive. Here you'll find his collection and that of other designers he likes as well as tableware, furniture, and books. His studio is upstairs, so you can find him in the shop from time to time.

207 BEST PACKING STORE

1-23-5 Aobadai
Meguro-ku ②
+81 (0)3-5773-5586
bestpackingstore.com

The theme of this shop is 'travel'. Everything in this shop is designed to make your journey more comfortable and some of the products on sale are originals. The kind of shop that makes you want to go on a trip, but many of the items can be used every day even when you are not travelling.

208 GOOD DESIGN SHOP
AT: GYRE, 2ND FL.

5-10-1 Jingumae
Shibuya-ku ③
+81 (0)3-3406-2323
d-department.com/jp/
shop/gooddesignshop

One of the D&D Department Project shops, created by the designer Kenmei Nagaoka, who collaborates with Comme des Garçons. They stock plenty of simple storage furniture as well as limited CdG products, that are only available here.

209 LA KAGU

67 Yaraicho
Shinjuku-ku ⑤
+81 (0)3-5227-6977
lakagu.com

The shop used to be a warehouse of Shinchosha, Japan's leading publishing house. Because the building remained vacant for 20 years, it has a certain authenticity that you won't find in newly-built shops. They sell products that will enrich your life – from fashion items to books and CDs. And they have an excellent cafe, too.

210 TSUTAYA ELECTRICS
AT: TERRACE MARKET, FUTAKO TAMAGAWA RISE

1-14-1 Tamagawa
Setagaya-ku ⑬
+81 (0)3-5491-8550
real.tsite.jp/futako
tamagawa

A consumer electronics shop, but not anything like the ones you'll find in Akihabara or Shinjuku. Here you shop for ultra-stylish electronics, as well as interior design items and books. The shop assistants are called 'concierges' and are experts in electronics.

The 5 best
INTERIOR DESIGN *shops*

---

211 **LOUNGE BY FRANCFRANC**

3-1-3 Minami-Aoyama
Minato-ku ④
+81 (0)3-5785-2111
francfranc.com

The flagship store of the popular interior design shop chain Francfranc. They sell products that will enrich your life, including their own original design range. Masterrecipe, one of their brands, offers simple but well-designed products that you can use for years. Fancy buying a towel made in Imabari?

212 **IDÉE**

2-16-29 Jiyugaoka
Meguro-ku ⑬
+81 (0)3-5701-7555
idee.co.jp

They originally started out as an imported furniture shop in 1975, but now they sell original, well-made furniture that lasts a lifetime. Their designs are timeless and add instant warmth to your interior. The Bakeshop, on the fourth floor, exudes the same fuzzy warmth.

213 **D&DEPARTMENT TOKYO**

8-3-2 Okusawa
Setagaya-ku ⑮
+81 (0)3-5752-0120
d-department.com

A 1000-square-metre emporium that stocks furniture, housewares, books, and CDs. Some of the products are second-hand. They also organise workshops, on knife sharpening for example, inviting professionals, and a farmer's market.

214 JOURNAL STANDARD FURNITURE

6-19-13 Jingumae
Shibuya-ku ③
+81 (0)3-6419-1350
js-furniture.jp

An interior design shop, which is run by the popular select shop Journal Standard. They sell a mix of trendy and vintage items from Japan and other countries. They also offer a full renovation service, and will even start by finding you a home. You can start with one room if you have no intention just yet of buying a home.

215 BAZAR ET GARDE-MANGER

5-2-11 Jingumae
Shibuya-ku ③
+81 (0)3-5774-5426
bazar-et-gm.com

All the items are selected by their French buyer Marthe Desmoulins, who used to own Absinthe in Paris. The shop's theme is 'a cabinet of curiosity'. The items Marthe selects are unique and cute and will add a fun twist to your interior.

215 BAZAR ET GARDE-MANGER

5 nice
C R A F T *shops*

---

216 TOKYU HANDS

12-18 Udagawacho
Shibuya-ku ①
+81 (0)3-5489-5111
tokyu-hands.co.jp

The department store of creative people's dreams, selling everything from stationery to hardcore DIY tools. The staff are knowledgeable and helpful. On the 6th floor, they stock a variety of fabrics and leathers. There is a cafe on the seventh floor. Easy to see how you could spend the whole day here…

217 YUZAWAYA

Yuzawaya
8-23-5 Nishi-Kamata
Ota-ku ⑭
+81 (0)3-3734-4141
yuzawaya.co.jp

If you are a keen knitter, then head over to this department store, which sells a variety of knitting yarns. They also have fabrics, beads, and other crafts goods. They sometimes organise free in-store craft workshops. Register online if you are interested.

218 OKADAYA

3-23-17 Shinjuku
Shinjuku-ku ⑦
+81 (0)3-3352-5411
okadaya.co.jp

A large craft shop in Shinjuku. Here they sell everything you need for crafts, including fabrics, buttons, and ribbons, as well as make-up goods for the stage and wigs. Some of the shop assistants can advise you on how to make your own costume for cosplay.

219 TOA

1-19-3 Jinnan
Shibuya-ku ①
+81 (0)3-3463-3351
toa-ltd.com

This fabric shop is stocked to the rafters with bargain items. Some of the fabrics often sell for less than 200 yen a metre. Most people go there to buy colourful fake fur. Fabrics with cute patterns, stylish and sophisticated textiles… a place that will fuel your creativity.

220 COCCA

1-31-13 Ebisu-Nishi
Shibuya-ku ②
+81 (0)3-3463-7681
cocca.ne.jp

A Japanese fabric brand as well as a shop that sells original fabrics. Their designs are an expression of a Japanese aesthetic that has existed for many decades. They organise sewing workshops from time to time. Don't worry if you are a beginner, the staff will gladly help you.

5 of the best
DEPA-CHIKA
(food halls)

---

221 ISETAN SHINJUKU STORE
3-14-1 Shinjuku
Shinjuku-ku ⑦
+81 (0)3-3352-1111
isetan.mistore.jp

Isetan Shinjuku is probably the busiest department store in Tokyo as several shops sell limited products there. The cookies by Fika, produced by Isetan Mitsukoshi Holdings, are especially popular. They are beautifully packed, making them the perfect gift.

222 HIKARIE
2-21-1 Shibuya
Shibuya-ku ①
+81 (0)3-3461-1090
hikarie.jp

Many of the products are only available from Hikarie but fortunately they are not as busy as Isetan. The basement cafe is overseen by the world's top barista Paul Bassett with Japan's leading patissier Yoshihiro Tsujiguhi. The only place in the world where you can find this combo of coffee and pastries.

223 IKEBUKURO SEIBU
1-28-1 Minami-Ikebukuro
Toshima-ku ⑪
+81 (0)3-3981-0111
sogo-seibu.jp/ikebukuro

Their food hall is huge. They even have guides on hand to point you in the right direction: 'delica attendant' and 'sweets attendant'. Just tell them what kind of deli food or sweets you are looking for and they will help you. There are eat-in spaces where you can have sushi, soba, or tempura.

224 TOKYU NORENGAI

2-24-1 Shibuya
Shibuya-ku ①
+81 (0)3-3477-3111
tokyu-dept.co.jp

In 1951, Japan's very first depa-chika, called Tokyu Norengai, opened. It reopened at the current location in 2013. It is connected to Tokyu Foodshow, another food market in the basement of Mark City. If you are interested in visiting one of Japan's long-established shops, then Norengai would be my choice.

225 GINZA SIX

6-10-1 Ginza
Chuo-ku ⑧
+81 (0)3-6891-3390
ginza6.tokyo

This food hall opened in 2017 and is possibly the most luxurious depa-chika in Japan, with world-famous shops and famous shops from all over Japan. Several of the products are 'only available at GINZA Six'. One of their most popular shops is the *noriben* (bento with rice covered with seasoned nori seaweed) shop. Join the line outside?

The 5 best
JAPANESE SWEET
shops

226 HIGASHIYA MAN

3-17-4 Minami-Aoyama
Minato-ku ④
+81 (0)3-5414-3881
higashiya.com

They have *Kashi* (sweets) that can be served with Japanese tea. They offer freshly steamed buns all through the year as well as *aisu monaka* (red bean ice cream in rice wafers) in summer and *oshiruko* (hot red bean soup) in winter.

227 QULOFUNE

1-24-11 Jiyugaoka
Meguro-ku ⑬
+81 (0)3-3725-0038
quolofune.com

Kasutera is a type of sponge cake made with flour, eggs and sugar. This Portuguese sweet was first introduced to Japan during the Edo period. Their *kasutera* is very airy with a fine texture, and their rusks, made of *kasutera*, are so crunchy that you won't stop at one.

228 MIZUHO

6-8-7 Jingumae
Shibuya-ku ③
+81 (0)3-3400-5483

Located on a back street in busy Harajuku, they sell only two things here: *mame daifuku*, *mochi* stuffed with red bean paste, and *monaka*, wafers filled with bean paste. Their *daifuku* is especially famous, and they often sell out before midday, even on weekdays.

229 KAMEJU

2-18-11 Kaminarimon
Taito-ku ⑩
+81 (0)3-3841-2210

Do you know the Japanese anime *Doraemon*? Do you remember what Doraemon likes to eat? *Dorayaki* of course! This snack is made with two small pancakes, stuffed with bean paste and is a popular sweet for Japanese people, but Kameju's *dorayaki* has a softer texture than others. There is always a line, but you'll find out soon enough that it's worth the wait.

230 KASHO SHOAN

1-9-20 Hiroo
Shibuya-ku ②
+81 (0)3-3441-1822

Their products are only sold at a few locations in Tokyo, which is why people often buy them as a gift when they visit people, friends and families outside Tokyo. *Anzu Daifuku*, mochi stuffed with red bean paste and apricot, is one of their signature products.

228 MIZUHO

The 5 best
PATISSERIES

231 TOSHI YOROIZUKA TOKYO
AT: KYOBASHI EDOGRAND

2-2-1 Kyobashi
Chuo-ku ⑧
+81 (0)3-6262-6510
grand-patissier.info

Patissier Toshi Yoroizuka was trained in Switzerland, Austria, France, and Belgium for eight years. He shot to fame soon after opening his first shop in 2004. He is very particular about ingredients and is even growing his own cacao beans to create the ultimate chocolate. You will not be able to resist his cakes.

232 AU BON VIEUX TEMPS

2-1-3 Todoroki
Setagaya-ku ⑬
+81 (0)3-3703-8428
aubonvieuxtemps.jp

One of the most renowned French patisseries by a Japanese patissier. Even French people who live in Tokyo recommend this shop. Their *gateaux secs* (biscuits) are very popular as a gift. They have an eat-in space where you can have lunch as well as cakes, of course.

233 GONDOLA

3-7-8 Kudan-Minami
Chiyoda-ku ⑤
+81 (0)3-3265-2761
patisserie-gondola.com

Their pound cake is widely considered the best in Tokyo. The shop opened over 80 years ago and its popularity has remained unchanged. As they are located in a business district, people often buy a box of their biscuits to present to clients.

234 SHIROTAE

4-1-4 Akasaka
Minato-ku ⑤
+81 (0)3-3586-9039

This shop opened in 1975 and its cheesecake proved a hit from the start. The 'rare' cheesecake, or unbaked cheesecake, is made with cream cheese, sugar, and lemon and nothing else. It is quite small but very filling because it is so rich. Their *choux à la crème* are also popular.

235 SEIKOTEI

2-30-3 Uehara
Shibuya-ku ⑬
+81 (0)3-3468-2178
seikotei.jp

Their boxes are beautifully illustrated with squirrels and are so cute that people often buy their products as a gift. The illustrations are by a Japanese female illustrator who has been drawing squirrels for them for over 15 years. The cookies in the boxes are simply delicious.

5 essential
INTERNATIONAL FOOD
stores

---

236 KINOKUNIYA INTERNATIONAL

3-11-7 Kita-Aoyama
Minato-ku ③
+81 (0)3-3409-1231
super-kinokuniya.jp

They opened as Japan's very first supermarket in 1953, selling a selection of products from all over the country as well as many imported foods and goods. Their in-store bakery sells a wide range of bread including German bread. Their original eco-bags are very robust and popular with customers.

237 NATIONAL AZABU

4-5-2 Minami-Azabu
Minato-ku ⑥
+81 (0)3-3442-3181
national-azabu.com

As this shop is located in an area where many expats live, you'll notice that they have many imported products you might not find at other stores. Since the 1960s, they have made the lives of many an expat in Tokyo much easier. About 70 % of their customers are not Japanese.

238 SEIJO ISHII

2-22-9 Ohashi
Meguro-ku
+81 (0)3-6416-8478
seijoishii.co.jp

The main store of this supermarket chain is located in Seijo, Setagaya-ku. They opened a larger branch in Ikejiri Ohashi in 2017, and soon everyone flocked there for their amazing stone oven baked pizza. Their cruffins or croissant muffins, which you can only buy here, are also popular.

239 VILLE MARCHE

2-13-5 Kita-Aoyama
Minato-ku ④
+81 (0)3-3403-1677
ville-marche.jp

This shop opened in 2016 and mainly sells organic products. They have a partnership with about 100 farmers from whom they source good quality seasonal products, and all of the agricultural products are traceable. They have an in-store bakery and freshly-brewed organic coffee. A good place to shop if you like healthy food.

240 KAWACHIYA SHOKUHIN

4-6-12 Ueno
Taito-ku ⑩
+81 (0)3-3831-2215
kawachiya-foods.com

Ameya Yokocho, aka Ameyoko, is an open-air market in Ueno and Kawachiya Shokuhin is one of the shops in the market. They import products from 30 countries around the world. If you're looking for a specific spice or herb, you may be able to find it here.

5
STALLS *and* FOOD TRUCKS
at the UNU *Farmer's Market*

Farmer's Market at Unu
5-53-70 Jingumae
Shibuya-ku ③

241 KAJUEN SHIRAKUMO

This orchard in Yamagata grows apples, and recently diversified, growing pears, plums, and Yamagata's speciality, cherries. They have chilled bottled apple juices which are a perfect thirst-quencher on a hot day. If you come across a grape variety called Dragon Ball, just buy it. It may be a bit expensive, but you won't regret your purchase.

242 KORIYAMA BRAND YASAI KYOGIKAI

brandyasai.jp

This farmers' cooperative believes in growing vegetables that taste good. The sweet corn and aubergine can be eaten raw while the sweet potatoes are as sweet as cakes without adding any sugar. Check their Facebook page as they are not always here.

241-245 **UNU FARMER'S MARKET**

242 **KORIYAMA BRAND YASAI KYOGIKAI**

めききのやさい、こおりやまから。
郡山ブランド野菜

unu.edu

243 BEBIBLE

bebible.jp

This is probably the first food truck you'll see when coming from Omotesando station. This highly popular food truck sells smoothies made with organic fruits and vegetables. Choose a water-based or dairy/soy milk based smoothie, to feel completely re-energised.

244 KOMESHIRUNA

Their van has been fitted with a firewood oven, which they use to cook rice and eggs, and grill meat. Have you ever tasted rice cooked in a stove instead of in an electric rice cooker? Try it with grilled pork, seasoned with salt and some sugar and nothing else.

245 PASADENA LUNCH WAGON

The owner fell in love with rotisserie chicken when he was travelling around the US. He uses local products as much as possible – for cooking but also for his biomass-fuelled truck. His chicken is very juicy even after it gets cold.

5

SPECIALIST SHOPS

246 **KIYA**

2-2-1 Nihonbashi
Muromachi
Chuo-ku ⑧
+81 (0)3-3241-0110
kiya-hamono.co.jp

This shop, which was established in the 16th century, sells top quality knives and scissors. They produce various chef's knives, from Japanese ones to Western and Chinese ones. Their gardening scissors and nail clippers are popular products. You can have your KIYA products sharpened here too.

247 **OKUNO KARUTA**

2-26 Kanda Jinbocho
Chiyoda-ku ⑨
+81 (0)3-3264-8031
okunokaruta.com

This shop specialises in Japanese playing cards, called *karuta*. *Karuta* derives from the Portuguese word *carta*, which were introduced in Japan by the Portuguese around the 1550s. This shop opened in 1921 and sells a variety of *karuta* and imported card games. They also regularly exhibit rare *karuta* sets.

248 **KAMAWANU**

23-1 Sarugakucho
Shibuya-ku ②
+81 (0)3-3780-0182
kamawanu.co.jp

This shop sells *tenugui*, or Japanese hand towels made of cotton. Japanese people can't do without *tenugui* in everyday life. They dry very quickly so they can be used as tea towels as well. You will be amazed by the variety of colourful and fashionable designs they sell.

249 HAIBARA

2-7-1 Nihonbashi
Chuo-ku ⑧
+81 (0)3-3272-3801
haibara.co.jp

This *washi* (traditional Japanese paper) shop opened in 1806. Of course, you can buy *washi* here but they also stock a variety of products made of *washi*, such as postcards, letter sets, and notebooks. *Chiyogami* (pattern-printed washi) is so beautiful that it wouldn't look out of place in a picture frame on a wall.

250 MATSUNEYA

2-1-10 Asakusabashi
Taito-ku ⑮
+81 (0)3-3863-1301
matsuneya.jp

A shop specialising in *sensu* (folding fan) and *uchiwa* (fan). The performers in the theatres in Asakusa and people who participate in festivals love their fans. If you're looking for more contemporary designs, look for the Showohdo brand, which was created by the current shop-keeper, a fourth-generation descendant of the shop's founder.

5 *interesting*
CD *and* VINYL SHOPS

---

251 **DISCLAND JARO**
26-6 Udagawacho
Shibuya-ku ①
+81 (0)3-3461-8256
music.geocities.jp/
disclandjaro

This shop, which opened in 1973, has always specialised in jazz. They have approximately 8000 records, mainly modern jazz, and you might come across some very rare discoveries in this tiny, ten-square-metre space. Please note that they do not accept credit cards.

252 **DISK UNION SHIBUYA**
AT: ANTENA21 BUILDING,
4TH FL.
30-7 Udagawacho
Shibuya-ku ①
+81 (0)3-3476-2627
diskunion.net

This shop has an extensive collection of used vinyl and CDs, mainly pop, jazz, and classical music. They regularly buy 60s and 70s rock records from overseas. If you're more into heavy metal, punk, and hard rock then head to the fifth floor. Probably the greatest selection in Tokyo.

253 **BONJOUR RECORDS**
24-1 Sarugakucho
Shibuya-ku ②
+81 (0)3-5458-6020
bonjour.jp

One of the landmarks of Daikanyama area. One of the first shops to combine music with fashion, selling records and CDs as well as clothes including items from their original brand. They also have a cafe on the ground floor. A good place to start to explore the area.

254 FACE RECORDS

10-2 Udagawacho
Shibuya-ku ①
+81 (0)3-3462-5696
facerecords.com

You may think that this is a clothes shop based on its façade but this is actually a used record shop with an excellent selection of 7-inch and 12-inch vinyl. They specialise in jazz, soul, reggae, and various other kinds of world music. If the shop isn't too crowded, the friendly shop assistants will let you listen to records.

255 JET SET TOKYO

2-33-12 #201 Kitazawa
Setagaya-ku ⑬
+81 (0)3-5452-2262
jetsetrecords.net

A popular shop with vinyl lovers as they produce records under their own label. The best place to score vinyl records by Japanese rock bands or hip-hop artists.

The 5 best

BOOKSHOPS

---

256 **AOYAMA BOOK CENTER**
AT: COSMOS AOYAMA GARDEN
FLOOR
5-53-67 Jingumae
Shibuya-ku ③
+81 (0)3-5485-5511
aoyamabc.jp

Possibly the best bookshop if you are looking for books on architecture, photography, and fine arts. Their shop is bright and airy, so you feel very comfortable while browsing their selection of books and magazines. They also organise small exhibitions and in-store events.

257 **HMV & BOOKS SHIBUYA**
1-21-3 Jinnan
Shibuya-ku ①
+81 (0)3-5784-3270
hmv.co.jp

HMV's first shop complex, located on the 5th, 6th and 7th floors of Shibuya MODI building, in the heart of Shibuya. Each level has an event space, and around 1000 events, including live music performances and talk shows, are organised here every year. They have a good selection of subculture books.

258 MORIOKA SHOTEN
AT: SUZUKI BUILDING, 1ST FL.
1-28-15 Ginza
Chuo-ku ⑧
+81 (0)3-3535-5020
takram.com

This bookshop sells only one title every week. They will display a particular book (which you can buy) and exhibit and sell related items in the shop. They often invite the author of the book they chose during that specific week. It is like a salon where authors, editors, and readers can gather around a specific book.

259 VILLAGE VANGUARD
2-10-5 Kitazawa
Setagaya-ku ⑫
+81 (0)3-3460-6145
village-v.co.jp

A bookshop chain, which is very popular with creative people and subculture fans, selling books and magazines as well as goods that are featured in magazines. But be warned: once you cross that doorstep, you might find it very difficult to drag yourself out of there and you may even end up breaking the bank.

260 DAIKANYAMA TSUTAYA BOOKS
17-5 Sarugakucho,
Shibuya-ku ②
+81 (0)3-3770-2525
real.tsite.jp/daikanyama

Tsutaya created the concept of a 'cultural convenience store' with the Daikanyama T-Site, which is a new type of cultural complex facility. Daikanyama Tsutaya is located in the centre of the site. The place to go for books, films, and music and the kind of shop where you could happily spend hours browsing.

5
STATIONERY
shops to check out

---

261 ITO-YA
2-7-15 Ginza
Chuo-ku ⑧
+81 (0)3-3561-8311
ito-ya.co.jp

Ito-ya, which opened in 1904, is a long-established stationery shop and reopened in 2015 after a renovation. The coffee counter on the ground floor starts serving at 8 am. You can buy and write postcards (you can even borrow a pen) in the Write & Post section on the second floor. There is even a post box!

262 LOFT
21-1 Udagawacho
Shibuya-ku ①
+81 (0)3-3462-3807
loft.co.jp

They sell a variety of products, including stationery as well as kitchen gadgets and interior design items but are mostly known for their amazing array of diaries and pens. From simple, practical ones to cute illustrated ones, they cater to every generation.

263 MARUZEN IKEBUKURO
AT: FUJIKYU EAST
NO.5 BUILDING
2-25-5 Minami-Ikebukuro
Toshima-ku ⑪
+81 (0)3-5962-0870
maruzenjunkudo.co.jp

This shop opened in August 2017 and is probably the largest stationery shop in Tokyo. Interestingly enough there are cab ends of two locomotives on the ground floor (which have nothing to do with stationery). The place to go if you're in the market for a fountain pen.

264 MISUZUDO

2nd Fl.
3-18-3 Kanda Nishikicho
Chiyoda-ku ⑨
+81 (0)3-5282-3265
misuzudo-b.com

Located on the second floor of the leading paper distribution company Takeo's showroom. They sell original notebooks in various sizes as well as handmade postcards and provide bookbinding service. They also organise one-day bookbinding workshops. The place to find gadgets for bookbinding.

265 GEKKOSO

8-7-2 Ginza
Chuo-ku ⑧
+81 (0)3-3572-5605
gekkoso.jp

An art supply store, which opened in 1917. They sell original paints (oil colour, watercolour, and gouache) and all the tools you need to paint. Every product features their horn logo. Their other original goods, such as pen cases and notebooks, are also very popular.

264 MISUZUDO

5

STATIONERY ITEMS

you should buy

266 **FRIXION PENS**

A series of erasable gel ink pens. There are 24 colours available in several thicknesses as well as highlighters, colour pencils, and stamps. They even have more professional models for businesspeople. Now that FriXion exists, kids no longer require correction fluid at school.

267 **DECORESE PENS**

A series of gel pens with a paint-like look and texture. A little bit like 3D. They come in lame and pastel colours and can be used on paper as well as plastic, glass, and metal. You can also use them for your nail art.

268 **MECHANICAL PENCILS**

Have you ever dreamed about a mechanical pencil with a lead that never breaks or doesn't need shaking for the lead to pop into place? They do exist. There is even a model with a rotating lead that sharpens itself every time you write. Japanese pencils are amazingly high tech.

269 COPIC MARKERS

Copic is a series of alcohol markers that are widely used by creative people including illustrators and architects. If you are not familiar with this series, you may want to consider buying the Copic Chao set of 36 colours. Then you can add other colours you like – there are 180 colours in all.

270 MASKING TAPE

Japanese people love to use masking tape as an alternative to Scotch tape but there are plenty of other fun uses. You can decorate a card, use it to stick a piece of paper in your diary, and so on. Some museum shops even sell special ones in the theme of their temporary exhibitions.

The 5 best
100 YEN / 300 YEN SHOPS

---

271 **DAISO HARAJUKU**

1-19-24 Jingumae
Shibuya-ku ③
+81 (0)3-5775-9641
daiso-sangyo.co.jp

The largest Daiso shop in Tokyo. If you are not familiar with Japan's 100 Yen shop concept, then start here. They have a variety of gifts for overseas tourists. It is known that talent scouts in the entertainment industry often stand in front of the shop in search of future actresses.

272 **SERIA**
AT: 17DIXSEPT, 3RD FL.

17-6 Daikanyamacho
Shibuya-ku ②
+81 (0)3-6416-1403
seria-group.com

Like the Daiso shop in Harajuku, this Seria shop is located in the heart of Daikanyama, one of the more fashionable areas in Tokyo. They have a good selection of products, catering to several generations. After spending time in this shop, there are plenty of places where you can have a coffee break nearby.

273 **CANDO**
AT: SEIBU SHINJUKU PEPE, 8TH FL.

1-30-1 Kabukicho
Shinjuku-ku ⑦
+81 (0)3-3202-1160
cando-web.co.jp

The largest Cando shop in Tokyo and the most extensive 100 Yen shop in Shinjuku area. The building is directly connected to Shinjuku Station, Seibu Shinjuku Line and is just a short walk from JR Shinjuku Station. They have a good selection of stationery.

274 **3COINS LUMINE EST SHINJUKU**
AT: LUMINE EST, 3RD FL.

3-38-1 Shinjuku
Shinjuku-ku ⑦
+81 (0)3-5363-0312
3coins.jp

Here every item costs less than 300 yen (+ the value added tax). Perhaps, their products are slightly cuter than the products in the 100 Yen shops. The accessories, including bags, hair clips, and earrings, do not look like they only cost 300 yen. They have a lot of useful kitchen gadgets as well.

275 **COUCOU**

2-11-6 Jiyugaoka
Meguro-ku ⑬
+81 (0)3-6421-1358
coucou.co.jp

Another 300 Yen shop, which is very popular with Japanese teenagers, who like to buy many of their original items including eco shoulder bags which sell like hotcakes and make a good gift for cycling fans. Their original kitchen gadgets are also worth checking out.

ASAKUSA CULTURE TOURIST INFORMATION CENTER

15 NOTABLE BUILDINGS

5 buildings
YOU CAN'T AFFORD TO MISS

—————

276 **NAKAGIN CAPSULE TOWER**
8-16-10 Ginza
Chuo-ku ⑧

Designed by Kisho Kurokawa, an iconic 20th-century architect, this building, which has 140 capsules, was built in 1972. This design is representative of the Metabolism trend in design, which describes the process of maintaining living cells.

277 **RYOTEI**
AT: KIYOSUMI GARDENS
3-3-9 Kiyosumi
Koto-ku ⑮
+81 (0)3-3461-5982

A *Sukiya-zukuri* style building, the style of which is influenced by the teahouse that was built in 1909 to welcome a British military leader of WWI, called Horatio Herbert Kitchener, during his inspection tour in Japan. Kiyosumi Teien is a leading example of a modern Japanese garden, and this *Ryotei* is a crucial element in it.

278 **JIYUGAKUEN MYONICHIKAN**
2-31-3 Nishi-Ikebukuro
Toshima-ku ⑪
+81 (0)3-3971-7535
jiyu.jp

This former school building was designed by one of the most famous American architects, Frank Lloyd Wright, in 1921. He received the commission while staying in Japan to design the Imperial Hotel. It is listed as a cultural property of national important. Along with the Imperial Hotel, this is widely regarded as Wright's most important work in Japan.

279 **SHIZUOKA SHIMNUN AND SHIZUOKA BROADCASTING SYSTEM BUILDING**

8-3-7 Ginza
Chuo-ku ⑧

This building is the Tokyo office of Shizuoka prefecture's regional newspaper and broadcasting companies. It was designed by Kenzo Tange and built in 1967. The design was influenced by the Metabolism trend. Catch a glimpse of it from the platform of JR Shimbashi Station while waiting for your train or even see it from the Yamanote Line.

280 **SEKIGUCHI CATHOLIC CHURCH / ST MARY'S CATHEDRAL**

3-16-15 Skiguchi
Bunkyo-ku ⑪
+81 (0)3-3945-0126
cathedral-sekiguchi.jp

This cathedral was also designed by Kenzo Tange. The previous building burnt down during WWII and was rebuilt with the support of the churches in Cologne, Germany, in 1964. From the outside, you would not guess that this is a church, but when seen from above, you realise that this is a cross-shaped building.

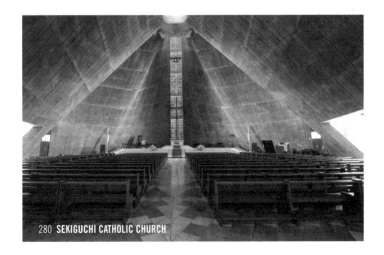

280 SEKIGUCHI CATHOLIC CHURCH

5 great examples of
MODERN ARCHITECTURE

---

281 PRADA

5-2-6 Minami-Aoyama
Minato-Ku ④
+81 (0)3-6418-0400
prada.com

Designed by the Swiss architects Herzog & de Meuron, this building really stands out in this area where you can shop for all the luxury brands. Don't forget to see it from the inside as well. You can also see the Miu Miu shop, designed by the same architects, through the rhomboid-shaped pattern on the façade.

282 MAISON HERMÈS

5-4-1 Ginza
Chuo-ku ⑧
+81 (0)3-3569-3300
maisonhermes.jp

Designed by Renzo Piano, this is the headquarters of Hermes Japon. During the day, the sun shines in through the glass façade, and at night, the same façade glows with the light from within. The Forum, on the eighth floor, hosts contemporary art exhibitions.

283 THE ICEBERG

6-12-18 Jingumae
Shibuya-ku ③

Designed by Creative Designers International, the Tokyo-based firm of the British architect Benjamin Warner. The concept behind the building's design is 'crystal cast out into an urban area'. It looks like an iceberg as the whole surface has a blueish metallic coating.

284 ASAKUSA CULTURE TOURIST INFORMATION CENTER

2-18-9 Kaminarimon
Taito-ku ⑩
+81 (0)3-3842-5566
city.taito.lg.jp

Designed by Kengo Kuma, an internationally-renowned Japanese architect. The building resembles seven tiers of wooden houses. Despite its very modern appearance, it blends in quite harmoniously with the surroundings. There is an observatory terrace on the eighth floor.

285 AOYAMA TECHNICAL COLLEGE

7-9 Uguisudanicho
Shibuya-ku ①
+81 (0)3-3463-0901
aoyamaseizu.ac.jp

You can study architecture and design at this professional technical college. Building 1 was designed by Makoto Sei Watanabe/ Architect's Office who won the international competition in 1988. It is sometimes referred to as 'Gundam Building', reminding people of the anime series.

281 PRADA

5 Buildings
BY TADAO ANDO

---

286 21_21 DESIGN SIGHT

9-7-6 Akasaka
Minato-ku ⑤
+81 (0)3-3475-2121
2121designsight.jp

Here people can broaden their understanding of design. The space is located in the Midtown Garden, right next to Hinokicho Park. You will somehow be inspired during your visit. In spring, you can also enjoy the cherry blossoms here.

287 OMOTESANDO HILLS

4-12-10 Jingumae
Shibuya-ku ③
+81 (0)3-3497-0310
omotesandohills.com

This building does not really look that special from the outside. Step inside, however, and you will soon be fascinated by its spiral ramp. This shopping centre was built on a wedge-shaped strip of land, forcing Ando to make the most of the land's features.

288 LA COLLEZIONE

6-1-3 Minami-Aoyama
Minato-ku ④
+81 (0)3-5468-1825
lacollezione.net

Built in 1989, this building consists of three cubes and one circular cylinder. Walking inside of the building, you may feel like as if you are lost in a maze but you will be amazed at the amount of daylight.
La Collezione is a multipurpose event space, which hosts press conferences and parties.

289 TOKYO ART MUSEUM

1-25-1 Sengawa-cho
Chofu-shi
+81 (0)3-3305-8686
tokyoartmuseum.com

This museum of fine arts, design and architecture opened in 2004 as part of an urban planning project in Sengawa. The area, about a five-minute walk from the station, is known as 'Sengawa Ando Street' and has several buildings designed by Ando.

290 BANK GALLERY

6-14-5 Jingumae
Shibuya-ku ③
+81 (0)3-6427-5834
bank-gallery.com

The building is located on 'Cat Street', a shopping street in Harajuku. It stands out because of its shape. It was originally built for Giorgio Armani's interior design showroom, but is now used as an events space, which mainly hosts art exhibitions.

286 21_21 DESIGN SIGHT

45 PLACES TO DISCOVER TOKYO

———

5 places for
HARUKI MURAKAMI FANS

---

291 AOYAMA
Minato-ku

Aoyama is, without doubt, the area that is most frequently associated with the author as he refers to it in his works quite often. It is referenced in one of the short stories in his recent collection *Men without Women* as well.

292 SENDAGAYA/GAIENMAE
Shibuya-ku/Minato-ku
④

If you have read his essays and interviews or articles about his life rather than his works, you may be aware that Murakami supports the Japanese baseball team, the Yakut Swallows. The Swallows' home stadium is located in this area, and sometimes he turns up for a game. Peter Cat, the jazz bar that he used to run, was also in the area.

293 YOTSUYA SANCHOME
Shinjuku-ku

In his latest work *Kishidancho Goroshi* (*Killing Commendatore*), the protagonist visits the area a few times as this is where his ex-wife works. Walk about 10 to 15 minutes to get to Yotsuya, which was featured in *Norwegian Wood*, where Toru and Naoko took a walk.

294 **KOKUBUNJI**
Kokunbunji-shi

He opened the jazz bar Peter Cat here, with his wife Yoko, when he was still at the university. Though it has since been renovated, there is an apartment called Maison Keyaki where he used to live. He probably never imagined he would one day be this famous while living there.

295 **HIROO**
Shibuya-ku/Minato-ku

Aomame, the protagonist of 1Q84, works at an expensive sports club in this area. It was also referenced in *Drive My Car*, one of the short stories in *Men without Women*. You can follow Aomame's footsteps towards the 'Willow House' or drive a car like the female driver did in the short story.

5 areas where you can see
OUTDOOR SCULPTURES

296 **ROPPONGI HILLS**
6-10-1 Roppongi
Minato-ku ⑥
+81 (0)3-6406-6000
roppongihills.com

There are several public artworks here: six works are overseen by the Mori Art Museum and three works were selected by the architect Fumihiko Maki. The eight-metre-tall rose, which was created by the German sculptor Iza Genzken, and Maman, by the French artist Louise Bourgeois, are definitely worth checking out.

297 **TOKYO MIDTOWN**
9-7-1 Akasaka
Minato-ku ⑤
+81 (0)3-3475-3100
tokyo-midtown.com

Art critic Toshio Shimizu and curator Jean-Hubert Martin selected artworks from artists all over the world. One of these works, called *Myomu* by the Hokkaido-born artist Kan Yasuda, welcomes you here in the space between Midtown East and West. There are several artworks inside the buildings as well.

298 **TOKYO INTERNATIONAL FORUM**
3-5-1 Marunouchi
Chiyoda-ku ⑧
+81 (0)3-5221-9000
t-i-forum.co.jp

There is one artwork on the site, called *Ishinki* and created by Kan Yasuda. He created several sculptures with the same name. There is another in Tokyo Midtown (but they are not the same shape). This work stands out between the geometric buildings.

299 MARUNOUCHI STREET GALLERY

Marunouchi Naka-dori
Chiyoda-ku ⑧

You can see several sculptures on Marunouchi Naka-Dori street, between the Tokyo International Forum and Tokyo Metro Otemachi station, and a few around the Mitsubishi Ichigokan Museum. The gallery was created in 1972 to enrich people's lives. The sculptures definitely make us feel more upbeat.

300 FUCHUNOMORI PARK

1-3-1 Sengencho
Fuchu-shi
+81 (0)42-364-8021

You'll find a large number of sculptures in this park, especially around the Fuchu Art Museum. Most of them are by prominent Japanese sculptors, including Yasutake Funakoshi and Churyo Sato. Don't forget to look out for *Jackass and Elephant*, a work by the British-born sculptor Bally Flanagan.

299 MARUNOUCHI STREET GALLERY

5 beautiful
GARDENS

---

301 RIKUGIEN GARDENS

6-16-3 Hon-Komagome
Bunkyo-ku ⑩
+81 (0)3-3941-2222

One of the best spots to see weeping cherry trees. Every year, at the end of March, the mesmerising blossoms attract huge crowds. But spring is not the only season you can enjoy this garden. Visit it in late November and you will be amazed by the bright red autumn leaves.

302 HAPPO-EN

1-1-1 Shirokanedai
Minato-ku ⑭
+81 (0)3-3443-3111
happo-en.com

People often book Happo-en for wedding ceremonies. You can also visit their garden, which has a tearoom where you can enjoy a cup of *matcha* with a seasonal Japanese sweet. Part of their building was apparently used as a model for Hayao Miyazaki's *Spirited Way*.

303 HAMARIKYU GARDENS

1-1 Hamarikyu Teien
Chuo-ku ⑮
+81 (0)3-3541-0200

One of the gardens used to be owned by a feudal lord during the Edo period. It is listed as a Japanese site of historic relevance and a place of scenic beauty. The water that runs through and around the garden comes directly from the sea. You may even spot jellyfish and other sea creatures swimming in it.

304 HANAHATA KINEN TEIEN
4-40-1 Hanahata
Adachi-ku

This garden was built to teach visitors about traditional Japanese culture. The rooms at Oukatei, the building in the garden, can be hired for a wedding, ikebana, and many other purposes. It has a surface area of over 9000 square metres, and somehow reminds us of a castle in the Edo period.

305 SHINJUKU GYOEN NATIONAL GARDEN
11 Naitomachi
Shinjuku-ku ⑦
+81 (0)3-3350-0151
env.go.jp/garden/shin-jukugyoen

A place where you can see flowers throughout the year, including cherry blossoms in spring, crape myrtles in summer, autumn leaves in hues of red and gold, and plum blossoms in winter. There are a restaurant and a tearoom inside the garden to satisfy those hunger pangs. Neither serves alcohol, however, as consuming alcohol in the garden is prohibited.

305 SHINJUKU GYOEN NATIONAL GARDEN

5

FREE OBSERVATORIES

---

306 TOKYO METROPOLITAN GOVERNMENT BUILDING OBSERVATION DECKS

2-8-1 Nishi-Shinjuku
Shinjuku-ku ⑦
+81 (0)3-5320-7890
metro.tokyo.jp

This observatory is located on the 45th floor of the Tokyo Metropolitan Government Office Building. It opens on weekends even though the offices are closed. A great place to enjoy unobstructed views of Tokyo from 202 metres above the ground. There is a direct lift to the observatory from the ground floor.

307 YEBISU GARDEN PLACE TOWER SKY LOUNGE

4-20 Ebisu
Shibuya-ku ②
+81 (0)3-5423-7111
gardenplace.jp

This observatory is located in Yebisu Garden Place, which is a complex of commercial facilities built on the site of a former beer brewery. The lounge is located on the 38th and 39th floors. On a clear day you may even be able to spot Mount Fuji.

308 HIKARIE

2-21-1 Shibuya
Shibuya-ku ①
+81 (0)3-5468-5892
hikarie.jp.e.ui.hp.transer.
com

Hikarie is situated in one of Tokyo's busiest areas, Shibuya. There is no real observatory here but you can visit the observation area on the 11th floor. From here, the town of Shibuya looks like a diorama. Open until midnight.

309 **BUNKYO CIVIC CENTER**
1-16-21 Kasuga
Bunkyo-ku ⑩
+81 (0)3-5803-1162

This facility is owned by Bunkyo City. On a beautiful day, you can see the skyscrapers in Shinjuku area as well as Mount Tsukuba and Mount Fuji. There is a restaurant, a cafe, and a concert hall in the same building.

310 **CARROT TOWER**
4-1-1 Taishido
Setagaya-ku ⑬

This free observatory is located on the 26th floor of a high-rise building, which you can enter from Sangenjaya Station. It is open until 11 pm and has a restaurant on the same floor so you can enjoy dinner with a view.

306 TOKYO METROPOLITAN GOVERNMENT BUILDING OBSERVATION DECKS

5
SAKE BREWERIES
you should visit

---

311 KOYAMA SHUZO

26-10 Iwabuchimachi
Kita-ku
+81 (0)3-3902-3451
koyamashuzo.co.jp

This *sakagura* (sake brewery), which was established in 1879, is the only one brewery in Tokyo's 23 special wards. Many sake breweries are located in remote mountain areas because pure water is an essential ingredient for sake. Their signature brand, Marushin Masamune, is a dry sake that pairs nicely with any type of cuisine.

312 TOSHIMAYA SHUZO

3-14-10 Kumegawacho
Higashimurayama-shi
+81 (0)42-391-0601
toshimayasyuzou.co.jp

They have been making sake here since 1596, during the Edo period. Their signature sake, Kinkon (which means 'golden wedding'), was launched on the occasion of the Meiji Emperor's silver wedding anniversary. You can buy Kinkon and other sake from their shop in Ochanomizu.

313 ISHIKAWA SHUZO

1 Kumagawa
Fussa-shi
+81 (0)42-553-0100
tamajiman.co.jp

This place styles itself as a 'theme park for sake lovers'. They offer a tour (available in English) so you can learn more about the sake brewing process and their buildings, parts of which are listed as cultural heritage. Don't forget to sample their sake, called Tamajiman, before leaving.

314 OZAWA SHUZO

2-770 Sawai
Ome-shi
+81 (0)42-878-8215
sawanoi-sake.com

They have been brewing sake here since 1702 and their signature brand, Sawanoi, is very well-known in Japan. You even have an opportunity to taste it during the brewery tour. Alternatively pop into one of the onsite restaurants. They also have a barbecue area.

315 TAMURA SHUZOJO

626 Fussa
Fussa-shi
+81 (0)42-551-0003
seishu-kasen.com

The Tamura family has been living in this area for over 400 years. In 1822, the ninth head of the family started to brew his own sake. In addition to their signature brand Kasen, they now also make Tamura, which was formulated by the current head of the family. Some parts of the brewery premises are listed as cultural heritage.

313 ISHIKAWA SHUZO

5 *spots to experience*
HOW CROWDED TOKYO IS

---

316 SHIBUYA SCRAMBLE CROSSING
Shibuya-ku ①

Everyone sooner or later ends up at this spot in Tokyo. An estimated 500.000 people use this crossing every day. The view from the Starbucks on the second floor of Shibuya Tsutaya, which faces the crossing, is quite amazing.

317 SHINJUKU STATION
Shinjuku-ku/Shibuya-ku ⑦

The most crowded station in the world, which is used by an estimated 760.000 people every day. JR, Tokyo Metro, Toei subway, Odakyu, and Keio all stop at this station. There are another two stations, Shinjuku Sanchome and Seibu Shinjuku, within walking distance. Easy to see why it is so crowded.

318 IKEBUKURO STATION
Toshima-ku ⑪

Ikebukuro is the second most crowded station around the world. The large Sunshine City shopping centre has an aquarium, planetarium, theatre, and museum. The Nanja Town and J-World Tokyo amusement parks, which are both run by Namco, are also nearby, which explains why it can be so busy.

319 TOKYO METRO TOZAI LINE

The congestion rate around 8 am between Kiba and Monzennakacho is a whopping 200%. It's difficult to explain what this feels like but imagine being in a crammed underground, with so many passengers around you that you can barely see the screen of your phone. Most people are exhausted before they even make it to the office.

320 JR SOBU LINE

The congestion rate shops short of 200% during the morning rush hour between Kinshicho and Ryogoku. Many people prefer to commute into work much earlier so they can actually find a seat on the train and relax. That said, this line is always pretty crowded during the rush hour.

316 SHIBUYA SCRAMBLE CROSSING

5 spots
TO SEE MOUNT FUJI

---

321 TAMAGAWA SENGEN SHRINE
1-55-12 Denen Chofu
Ota-ku ⑭
+81 (0)3-3721-4050
sengenjinja.info

Sengen Shrine was built more than 800 years ago during the Kamakura period. This ancient shrine is associated with the culture of faith relating to Mount Fuji and the mountain's spirit in particular. It is actually situated on an ancient burial mound, and a good place to enjoy a beautiful view of the mountain on a clear day.

322 FUJIMI BRIDGE
Setagaya-ku ⑫

Many people visit this bridge in Seijo Gakuen, Setagaya-ku in early February because you can see 'diamond Fuji'. This stunning natural phenomenon occurs when the sun aligns with the summit of Mount Fuji at sunrise or sunset, causing the mountain to shine bright like a diamond.

323 HANEDA AIRPORT INTERNATIONAL PASSENGER TERMINAL
2-6-5 Haneda Kuko
Ota-ku ⑭
+81 (0)3-6428-0888
haneda-airport.jp/inter

You'll catch plenty of plane spotters on the observation deck but it is also a good place for an unobstructed view of Mount Fuji. Realistically speaking, you should be able to see it from anywhere in Tokyo but the tall buildings often tend to get in the way. The view from Terminal 1 is also quite good.

324 **RAINBOW BRIDGE**
Minato-ku (14) (15)

This 798-metre-long bridge was opened to connect Shibaura with Odaiba in 1993. You can cross the bridge by car or use the Yurikamome, a driverless, automated transit service. There is also a free footpath. You might run into people with a tripod who are trying to get a perfect shot of Mount Fuji.

325 **FUJIMI TERRACE**
AT: HIGASHI KURUME STATION
1-8 Higashi-Honcho
Higashikurume-shi

You may have seen a lot of places that are called 'Fujimi' and wonder what this means. This roughly translates as 'gazing at Mount Fuji', so anytime a place is called 'Fujimi' it is, or used to be, a spot from where you could observe this famous mountain. The view from this terrace was selected as one of the 100 best views of Fuji in Kanto.

324 MOUNT FUJI SEEN FROM RAINBOW BRIDGE

The 5 most attractive
NATURAL HOT SPRINGS

---

326 MIYAGIYU

2-18-11 Nishi-Shinagawa
Shinagawa-ku ⑭
+81 (0)3-3491-4856
miyagiyu.co.jp

A natural hot spring bath house near Shinagawa. Their hot spring naturally contains metasilicic acid which is said to beautify your skin. One of their two baths is on the rooftop, meaning you can gaze at the stars while enjoying a relaxing bath and getting lost in your thoughts. The men's and women's baths are replaced every week.

327 MYOJIN-NO-YU

1-18-1 Oyata
Adachi-ku
+81 (0)3-5613-2683
myoujin-no-yu.com

This *onsen* has several types of baths, a sauna, a massage parlour, and a restaurant (this is what we call a 'super sento'). The largest bath contains plenty of iron and salt, and is said to improve dermatological ailments. They provide rental body and hand towels.

328 JAKOTSUYU

1-11-11 Asakusa
Taito-ku ⑩
+81 (0)3-3841-8645
jakotsuyu.co.jp

Located in the heart of Asakusa, near Senso-ji, this bath house has been popular with the locals since the Edo period. The water contains metasilicic acid and bicarbonate soda. They sell towels at an affordable price so you don't have to bring your own.

329 SHIMIZUYU

3-9-1 Koyama
Shinagawa-ku ⑭
+81 (0)3-3781-0575
shimizuyu.com

They have two springs here, the golden and the black spring. The water of the former is brought up from 1500 metres below the ground, from a layer that dates from the Pleistocene and contains enriched natural iodine. The latter one contains bicarbonate soda and plenty of minerals and is brought up from 200 metres. Both baths soften and moisturise your skin.

330 SAYA-NO-YUDOKORO

3-41-1 Maenocho
Itabashi-ku
+81 (0)3-5916-3826
sayanoyudokoro.co.jp

The pale green water in this bath house is pumped up straight from the source and is considered effective for those who suffer from neuralgia, muscle and joint pain, skin ailments and so on. There is a restaurant that serves soba noodles, made of 100% buckwheat without wheat flour.

5

TOILETS

worth checking out

---

331 HIKARIE
2-21-1 Shibuya
Shibuya-ku ①
+81 (0)3-5468-5892
hikarie.jp

The toilets at Hikarie are called Switch Rooms and they are not your usual run-of-the-mill toilets. There are six of them, and each one has a different concept with different lighting, BGM, and scent. If you have small kids with you, go to Mummy's STAGE in the basement (B2). Dad can use it, too.

332 HIGASHIYA GINZA
AT: POLA GINZA BUILDING,
2ND FL.
1-7-7 Ginza
Chuo-ku ⑧
+81 (0)3-3538-3230
higashiya.com/ginza

With a combination of black stone and plain wood, these women's toilets, and the wash basin especially, are just gorgeous. You will have to eat at the restaurant to use it but the experience is certainly worth it. Consider ordering a cup of tea and a piece of *yokan*, perhaps.

333 MANDARIN ORIENTAL TOKYO
2-1-1 Nihonbashi
Muromachi
Chuo-ku ⑧
+81 (0)3-3270-8800
mandarinoriental.co.jp/
tokyo

This hotel is located on floors 30 through 38 of the Nihonbashi Mitsui Tower and their lobby is on the 38th floor. So, if you have a chance to visit it, when you are staying or dining there, then do check out their toilet. People call it the 'toilet in the sky'.

334 LUMINE IKEBUKURO

1-11-1 Nishi-Ikebukuro
Toshima-ku ⑪
+81 (0)3-5954-1111
lumine.ne.jp/ikebukuro

Many people tend to use the toilets on the basement level of this building. But if you have some time to spare, then make the trek to the women's toilets on the 6th floor (sorry, guys). It is very bright and has plenty of space so you can touch up your make-up. In fact, you may even end up staying longer than you intended.

335 HOTEL GAJOEN TOKYO

1-8-1 Shimo-Meguro
Meguro-ku ⑭
+81 (0)3-3491-4111
hotelgajoen-tokyo.com

This hotel is considered to be one of most gorgeous places in the East and the same can definitely be said of their toilets, which resemble a tiny Japanese garden with a vermillion-lacquered bridge over a stream. The doors are decorated with mother-of-pearl while Japanese paintings cover the ceiling.

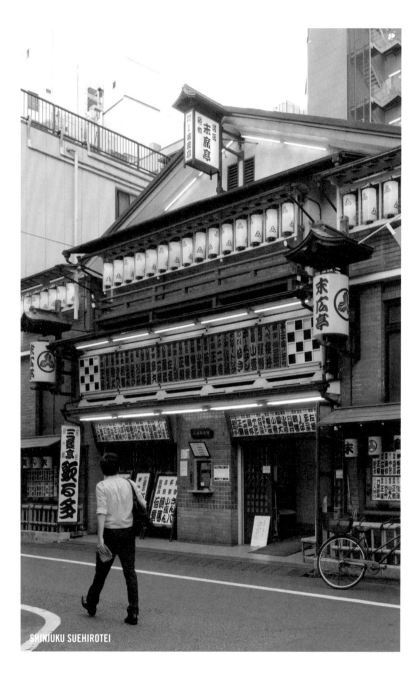

SHINJUKU SUEHIROTEI

55 PLACES
TO ENJOY CULTURE

The 5 most beautiful
SHRINES and TEMPLES

---

336 MANGANJI TEMPLE TODOROKI FUDOSON
1-22-47 Todoroki
Setagaya-ku ⑬
+81 (0)3- 3701-5405
manganji.or.jp

Located close to Todoroki Keikoku, the only gorge in Tokyo's 23 wards, and a popular spot for *takigyo* or waterfall training. The more than 150 cherry trees here make for fantastic viewing spring. Stop for an ice cream at Shiki no Hana before leaving.

337 YASUKUNI SHRINE
3-1-1 Kudan-Kita
Chiyoda-ku ⑤
+81 (0)3-3261-8326
yasukuni.or.jp

This shrine was built by order of the Meiji Emperor in the late 19th century as a foundation for a peaceful Japan. There are major controversies surrounding this shrine, but let us forget about these for now and enjoy its beauty and the scenery of the cherry blossoms in spring and the red foliage in autumn.

338 GOHYAKURAKANJI
3-20-1 Shimo-Meguro
Meguro-ku ⑭
+81 (0)3-3792-6751
rakan.or.jp

Rakan, or *arakan*, is called *arhat* in English and is a disciple of Buddha. At this temple, there are more than 300 statues of *arhat*. They are supposed to represent the 500 disciples who gathered at the death of Buddha. It is quite amazing to see such a large number of Buddhist statues gathered in one place.

339 KAMEIDO TENJIN

**3-6-1 Kameido
Koto-ku ⑮**
+81 (0)3-3681-0010
kameidotenjin.or.jp

There are more than 300 plum trees at this shrine, which are tended by Shinto priests. Ume Matsuri, or the Plum Festival, is held here from February to March when the trees are in blossom. The shrine is also known as a wonderful spot to see the wisteria flower in late April.

340 ZENPUKUJI

**1-6-21 Moto-Azabu
Minato-ku ⑥**
+81 (0)3-3451-7402
azabu-san.or.jpx

This temple was built in the 9th century, making it the third oldest temple in Tokyo. There is a huge 750-year-old gingko tree here with unusual branches, which all look like they are hanging down.

336 MANGANJI TEMPLE TODOROKI FUDOSON

5 places for
JAPANESE
TRADITIONAL CULTURE

---

341 **KABUKI-ZA THEATRE**
4-12-5 Ginza
Chuo-ku ⑧
+81 (0)3-3545-6800
kabuki-za.co.jp

This is one of the theatres where you can still attend traditional Kabuki performances. This unique Japanese theatre is over 400 years old. You can also enjoy a *bento* during the intermission. If you have a balcony seat, you can order a special bento, which will be delivered to your seat.

342 **NATIONAL THEATRE**
4-1 Hayabusacho
Chiyoda-ku ⑤
+81 (0)3-3265-7411
ntj.jac.go.jp

Here you can see Kabuki, Noh, and Bunraku performances. The National Engei Hall, where you can enjoy storytelling performances, such as *rakugo*, *kodan*, and *rokyoku*, is located next to the National Theatre. There is also an exhibition space which showcases objects used in these traditional performing arts.

343 **KANZE NOH THEATRE**
AT: GINZA SIX
6-10-1 Ginza
Chuo-ku ⑧
+81 (0)3-6274-6579
kanze.net

One of the Noh theatres in Tokyo, which opened in 2017 in the basement of the Ginza Six commercial complex. Though it does not have any eating facilities, there are plenty of restaurants in the building and nearby. Check out their range of merchandise, which you can only buy here.

344 KIOI SMALL HALL

6-5 Kioicho
Chiyoda-ku ⑤
+81 (0)3-5276-4500
kioi-hall.or.jp

A concert hall for Japanese traditional music. The musicians play the *koto*, *shamisen*, and other traditional instruments and are sometimes accompanied by dancers. The hall, which can accommodate up to 250 people, is so small you can hear and almost feel the musicians breathing.

345 SHINJUKU SUEHIROTEI

3-6-12 Shinjuku
Shinjuku-ku ⑦
+81 (0)3-3351-2974
suehirotei.com

A venerable entertainment hall where traditional *rakugo* storytelling performances are given. Nowadays you can take in a *rakugo* performance almost anywhere, but this long-established theatre has been open since 1897 and is a great place to learn more about the world of *Showa Genroku Rakugo Shinju*, a serialised anime. You can bring food and drinks (but no alcohol).

341 KABUKI-ZA THEATRE

5 museums about
JAPANESE ART

---

346 NEZU ART MUSEUM
6-5-1 Minami-Aoyama
Minato-ku ④
+81 (0)3-3400-2536
nezu-muse.or.jp

The Japanese and oriental art collection of the businessman and politician Kaichiro Nezu (1860-1940). The museum reopened in 2009 after a three-year renovation. Take a walk in the lovely garden after visiting the collection for a break from the city in the city.

347 YAMATANE MUSEUM OF ART
3-12-36 Hiroo
Shibuya-ku ②
+81 (0)3-5777-8600
(NTT Hello Dial)
yamatane-museum.jp

This museum, which opened in 1966, specialises in Japanese art. Their collection includes several works that are listed as 'Important Cultural Properties', and which were created by Kagaku Murakami, Gyoshu Hayami, and several other leading artists. There is a cafe near the entrance where you can enjoy seasonal Japanese sweets.

348 OTA MEMORIAL MUSEUM OF ART
1-10-10 Jingumae
Shibuya-ku ③
+81 (0)3-5777-8600
(NTT Hello Dial)
ukiyoe-ota-muse.jp

Though this is not a large museum, it has an exciting collection of over 14.000 woodblock prints or *ukiyo-e*, including work by Hokusai and Hiroshige. During the summer, they usually host thematic exhibitions of ghost and monster prints.

349 **IDEMITSU MUSEUM OF ART**
AT: TEIGEKI BUILDING, 9TH FL.
3-1-1 Marunouchi, Chiyoda-ku ⑧
+81 (0)3-5777-8600
(NTT Hello Dial)
idemitsu-museum.or.jp

This museum has a superb Japanese art collection, including *suiboku-ga* (monochrome ink painting) and Rimpa School paintings as well as Japanese calligraphy. The premises were designed by the architect Yoshio Taniguchi (who also designed an addition to the MoMA in NYC). One of the rooms originally was a tearoom and is now used as a gallery to display tea-making utensils.

350 **SEN-OKU HAKUKO KAN MUSEUM**
1-5-1 Roppongi Minato-ku ⑥
+81 (0)3-5777-8600
(NTT Hello Dial)
sen-oku.or.jp/Tokyo

This museum, also known as the Sumitomo Collection, houses the collection of the family that founded this Japanese industrial conglomerate. The family has two museums. The other one is in Kyoto. The Tokyo museum exhibits utensils for the tea ceremony, ceramic art, Buddhist art, Noh masks and modern Japanese paintings.

346 NEZU ART MUSEUM

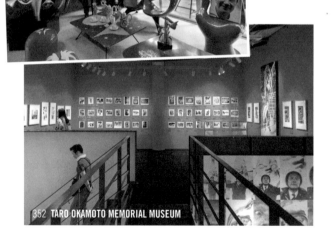

352 TARO OKAMOTO MEMORIAL MUSEUM

5 interesting
SMALL MUSEUMS

351 **KUMAGAI MORIKAZU MUSEUM**
2-27-6 Chihaya
Toshima-ku ⑪
+81 (0)3-3957-3779
kumagai-morikazu.jp

Morikazu Kumagai was a 20th-century Japanese artist. The museum was built on the site where he lived for 45 years. His highly-recognisable oil paintings of animals in bright colours are very popular. The museum also has a nice cafe, called Kaya, after Kumagai's daughter, on the ground floor.

352 **TARO OKAMOTO MEMORIAL MUSEUM**
6-1-19 Minami-Aoyama
Minato-Ku ④
+81 (0)3-3406-0801
taro-okamoto.or.jp

"Art is an explosion!" Taro Okamoto will forever be remembered for this quote and *The Tower of the Sun* in Osaka. This small museum displays many of the artist's works. It also has an excellent cafe, called Piece of Cake, where you can eat and drink while you admire his sculptures.

353 **THE NURIE MUSEUM**
4-11-8 Machiya
Arakawa-ku
+81 (0)3-3892-5391
nurie.jp

This museum exhibits colouring books from overseas and Japan but mainly focusses on the works of Kiichi Tsutaya, whose colouring books took Japan by storm from around 1945 to 1955. Japan's kawaii culture has its roots in his pictures. There is also a space where you can colour pictures. Have fun!

354 THE SHOTO MUSEUM OF ART

2-14-14 Shoto
Shibuya-ku ①
+81 (0)3-3465-9421
shoto-museum.jp

This art museum is located in a quiet residential area called Shoto. While the museum has no collection of its own, they do host amazing small exhibitions. Head over to one of the many places nearby after your visit as the museum has no cafe. Definitely a must-see during your stroll through Shibuya.

355 YAYOI MUSEUM

2-4-3 Yayoi
Bunkyo-ku ⑩
+81 (0)3-3812-0012
yayoi-yumeji-museum.jp

This museum has an extensive collection of book illustrations, including works by Kiyokata Kabyraki and Junichi Nakahara. The Takehisa Yumeji Museum next door exhibits the works of Takehisa, an artist whose work is representative of the Taisho period. The museum shop has a nice collection of original items.

5

UNUSUAL MUSEUMS

356 **SUGINAMI ANIMATION MUSEUM**
AT: SUGINAMI KAIKAN, 3RD FL.
3-29-5 Kamiogi
Suginami-ku
+81 (0)3-3396-1510
sam.or.jp

A museum for die-hard anime fans where they can learn more about anime history and enjoy old anime movies. The permanent exhibition includes recreations of the works of well-known animators. The museum also hosts anime workshops for kids where they can create their own. Check out the autographs of the many manga artists and voice actors near the entrance to the third floor.

357 **TOKYO SOME-MONO-GATARI MUSEUM**
3-6-14 Nishi-Waseda
Shinjuku-ku ⑪
+81 (0)3-3987-0701

This museum is located in Tomita Senkogei, a kimono workshop. They have been dyeing textile here since the Meiji period. The exhibits feature tools used for dyeing. The museum also organises workshops where you can learn to make *Edo Komon*, or stencil patterns.

メダマイカリムシ

節を魚の眼の中に
入れて寄生する甲殻類

358 PAPER MUSEUM
AT: ASUKAYAMA PARK
1-1-3 Oji
Kita-ku
+81 (0)3-3916-2320
papermuseum.jp

This museum, which opened in 1950, collects and exhibits documents on Japanese handmade washi paper and paper that was made overseas. Learn more about papermaking, paper recycling, and the history of washi and other handmade papers. The garden is just as instructive as it is full of plants that are used for papermaking.

359 PRINTING MUSEUM
1-3-3 Suido
Bunkyo-ku ⑩
+81 (0)3-5840-2300
printing-museum.org

One of the largest printing companies in Japan, called Toppan Printing, founded this museum in 2000 to commemorate its centenary. It is dedicated to the history and techniques of printing and also hosts temporary exhibitions of beautiful books and posters.

360 MEGURO PARASITO-LOGICAL MUSEUM
4-1-1 Shimo-Meguro
Meguro-ku ⑭
+81 (0)3-3716-1264
kiseichu.org

Biologist Satoru Kamegai created this museum, which hosts exhibitions about parasitic insects and conducts research on them. Unless you are an expert in this field, every display has new surprises in store for you. A rather unique museum.

5 must-do's
AT KOKUGIKAN

Kokugikan
1-3-28 Yokoami
Sumida-ku ⑬
+81 (0)3-3623-5111
sumo.or.jp

361 GREET RIKISHI

Would you like to see *rikishi* (sumo wrestlers) up close? Then wait for them near the west entrance. Only *Yokozuna* and *Ozeki*, the two highest ranks, can use cars to get to Kokugikan (so you are unlikely to see them). The *rikishi* of other ranks must walk there. Be there around 2 pm.

362 EAT CHANKO AND YAKITORI

Rikishi eat *chanko*, a type of soup. The recipes vary, depending on the schools or the cooks. During tournaments, the schools take turns serving their *chanko* in the basement. *Yakitori* (grilled chicken skewers with a soy-based sauce) are probably the most famous snack at this venue.

363 VISIT SUMO MUSEUM

You can visit this museum if you have a ticket to a tournament. Learn everything there is to know about *sumo*, and in particular about the history of this noble sport. The exhibit changes every two months so visitors have good reason to return.

364 TAKE PURIKURA

Purikura, aka Print Club, is a photo booth where you can create your own photo stickers to take home as a souvenir. At Kokugikan, you can create a sheet of stickers of you and the *yokozuna* (and your friends as long as all of you fit in the booth). This machine is unique to the stadium.

365 BUY GOODS

There are several shops in Kokugikan. And some of the staff are larger than life. These retired *rikishi* now work for the Sumo Association as shop assistants. Some of the original merchandise is very practical, such as the *tenugui* (hand towel) and notebooks.

361 GREET RIKISHI

5 essential places for
MANGA and **ANIME**
LOVERS

366 DICE IKEBUKURO
1-11-11 Higashi-
Ikebukuro
Toshima-ku ⑪
+81 (0)3-5944-9202
diskcity.co.jp

DiCE Ikebukuro is the largest *manga kissa*, which is similar to an Internet cafe, in Tokyo. They stock about 180.000 manga titles on eight floors. Like Internet cafes, they have PCs, shower rooms, and bars. They even have an ice-cream machine (can be used without additional charge!) and a karaoke facility.

367 JUMP SHOP
1-3-61 Koraku
Bunkyo-ku ⑩
+81 (0)3-5842-6844
*shonenjump.com/j/
jumpshop/*

The shop of the Shonen Jump manga magazine. You can buy a variety of items illustrated with popular characters as well as comics. Some of them are only available from this shop. The shop's character Junta was created by Akira Toriyama, the creator of *Dragon Ball*.

368 KITARO CHAYA
5-12-8 Jindaiji
Motomachi
Chofu-shi
+81 (0)42-482-4059

Ge GE Ge no Kitaro is a popular manga and anime series, which was created in 1960. The characters of the series welcome you in the cafe where you can enjoy an original menu. See illustrations by the series' author, Shigeru Mizuki, on the second floor.

369 TOKIWASO-DORI OYASUMIDOKORO

2-3-2 Minami-Nagasaki
Toshima-ku ⑪
+81 (0)3-6674-2518

Tokiwaso is a block of flats that was built in the fifties and demolished in 1982. Several famous manga artists, such as Osamu Tezuka, Fujio Fujiko (both of them), Shotaro Ishimori, and Fujio Akatsuka lived here. Now there is just a monument to remind you that the building once stood here. You can still visit many of the places frequented by the artists in the area.

370 NAKANO BROADWAY

5-52 Nakano
Nakano-ku ⑫

A must-see if you want to experience Tokyo's subculture. Here you can find newly-published manga in rare first editions as well as figures and trading cards. You may find collectibles of anime characters that you used to watch on TV when you were a kid. Very pricy.

370 NAKANO BROADWAY

5

SPOTS *you may have seen*
in FILMS

---

371 **JOUGANJI TEMPLE**
2-26-6 Honcho
Nakano-ku ⑫
+81 (0)3-3372-2711
nakanojouganji.jp

This is the temple Charlotte, played by Scarlett Johansson, visits when wandering around Tokyo in Sofia Coppola's *Lost in Translation*. This photogenic temple was built approximately 650 years ago. Spring is probably the best season to visit as there are weeping cherry trees on either side of the gate.

372 **UENO PEDESTRIAN DECK**
Near Ueno Station
Taito-ku ⑩

This place was featured in James Mangold's *The Wolverine*. Logan, played by Hugh Jackman, and Mariko, played by TAO, catch the bullet train to Osaka here. In reality, the trains to Osaka depart from Tokyo Station, not Ueno.

373 **THE CREST TOWER**
2-11-6 Tsukuda
Chuo-ku ⑮

In Alejandro González Iñárritu's *Babel*, Chieko Wataya, a deaf Japanese teenage girl played by Rinko Kikuchi, lives in a high-rise apartment with her father. Their apartment was in this building. Many similar high-rise buildings were built in this area in recent years.

374 **SUGA SHRINE**
5 Sugacho
Shinjuku-ku ⑤
+81 (0)3-3351-7023
sugajinjya.org

Seichi junrei, literally meaning 'pilgrimage', is a term that is mainly used by anime fans who like to visit the places that are featured in their favourite manga. This shrine was shown in an anime called *Your Name*. (Japanese title: *Kimi no Na wa*) by Makoto Shinkai. As the film became a blockbuster hit, many people have since visited the place to 'worship' it.

375 **YANAGIBASHI BRIDGE**
Near Asakusabashi
Station
Higashi-Nihonbashi,
Chuo-ku ⑮
Yanagibashi, Taito-ku

Yanagibashi is a bridge over the Kanda River, just before its confluence with the Sumida River. This bridge was featured in the Japanese horror film *The Grudge* by Takashi Shimizu. The university professor Peter sees it from the balcony. This bridge is also a familiar feature in TV dramas.

372 UENO PEDESTRIAN DECK

The 5 most interesting
F E S T I V A L S
to catch

---

376 SANJA MATSURI
AT: ASAKUSA SHRINE
2-3-1 Asakusa
Taito-ku ⑩
+81 (0)3-3844-1575
asakusajinja.jp

This *matsuri* (festival) takes place every year in May at the Asakusa Shrine, which is also called Sanja-sama, one of the most famous Shinto shrines in the city. During the festival, portable *mikoshi* (miniature shrines) are carried around in processions by the neighbourhood associations in honour of the three founders of the Sensoji Temple.

377 KAGURAZAKA MATSURI
Kagurazaka area
Shinjuku-ku

In July, Awa-odori dancers flood the streets of Tokyo, in a frenzied spectacle as they parade through Kagurazaka. This is a great opportunity to experience this traditional area of the city. One of the verses of the song to which they dance says: 'A dancing fool and a watching fool. If both are fools, then you're better off dancing'. Fancy a dance?

378 **TOUROU NAGASHI**
Asakusa area
Taito-ku
+81 (0)3-3844-1221

In mid-August, during o-bon (one of the Buddhist rituals), we release candle-lit lanterns into the Sumida River to commemorate the souls of the people who died in the Sumida River during the Great Kanto Earthquake and the Great Tokyo Air Raids. Everyone can buy a lantern to join.

379 **FUKAGAWA HACHIMAN MATSURI**
AT: TOMIOKA HACHIMANGU SHRINE
1-20-3 Tomioka
Koto-ku ⑮
+81 (0)3-3642-1315
tomiokahachimangu.or.jp

This is one of the three festivals in Tokyo that takes place around 15 August, and the most important event at the shrine. During *Hon-matsuri*, which takes place once in every three years, you can see a procession of 120 *mikoshi* or portable shrines. A few of the *mikoshi* are decorated with real gold and diamonds. Worth seeing!

380 **AZABU JUBAN SUMMER NIGHT FESTIVAL**
Azabu Juban area
Minato-ku ⑥

Every year in August. Though it was scaled down a few years ago, this festival still attracts a great many visitors. The area is known to have a variety of excellent restaurants, and these restaurants have stalls at the festival to offer their specialities at reasonable prices.

5

FIREWORKS

festivals not to miss

---

381 ADACHI NO HANABI
ADACHI FIREWORKS FESTIVAL
**Riverbed of the
Arakawa River
Adachi-ku**

Every year in July the fireworks festival season kicks off with this festival. They launch around 12.000 fireworks over an hour, ending with 'Niagara', a fireworks display in the shape of a waterfall. Head to Nishi-Ari for a breath-taking view of the Niagara.

382 EDOGAWA HANABI TAIKAI
EDOGAWA FIREWORKS
FESTIVAL
**Riverbed of the
Edogawa River
Edogawa-ku**

The festival is also called 'Exciting Fireworks Festival' and is takes place in August. It begins with a jaw-dropping spectacular of 1000 fireworks, that are launched in just five seconds (Yes, that's right, five seconds) followed by special displays, which change every year. This festival is the biggest crowd-puller.

383 ITABASHI HANABI TAIKAI
ITABASHI FIREWORKS
FESTIVAL
**Riverbed of the
Arakawa River
Itabashi-ku**
itabashihanabi.jp

This festival is held in August in collaboration with Toda City, Saitama, which is located on the opposite side of the river. About 12.000 fireworks are fired into the sky, making for a good show. There are some paid seats if you want to be certain that you'll have a good view.

384 SUMIDAGAWA HANABI TAIKAI

SUMIDAGAWA FIREWORKS FESTIVAL

Riverbed of the Sumida River Sumida-ku/Taito-ku
sumidagawa-hanabi.com

This festival was first organised in 1733. It is divided into two areas, and the sky is ablaze with dazzling colour from around 22.000 fireworks. A fireworks competition is held in one of the areas, with ten groups competing every year. Avoid the crowds by buying a ticket for a sightseeing boat to enjoy the spectacle from the water.

385 JINGU GAIEN HANABI TAIKAI

JINGU GAIEN FIREWORKS FESTIVAL

Jingu Gaien area Kasumigaokamachi/ Shinjuku-ku ④
jinguhanabi.com

The first festival was held in 2011 to raise funds in the wake of the Great East Japan Earthquake and since then it has been organised in August every year. Live music concerts, with a line-up of twenty bands, are held at the two baseball stadiums. Don't forget to buy tickets.

385 JINGU GAIEN FIREWORKS FESTIVAL

5 great
NIGHTCLUBS

---

386 **UNIT**
AT: ZA HOUSE BUILDING
1-34-17 Ebisu-Nishi
Shibuya-ku ②
+81 (0)3-5459-8630
unit-tokyo.com

They host club events and gigs here almost every night and are known for their excellent sound system. With plenty of legendary events in recent years, with musicians and DJs from Japan and overseas, this is the place to go if you want to enjoy an epic night.

387 **CONTACT**
AT: SHINTAISO BUILDING NO. 4
2-10-12 Dogenzaka
Shibuya-ku ①
+81 (0)3-6427-8107
contacttokyo.com

Since its opening in 2016, Contact has already welcomed many world-famous DJs, such as Gilles Peterson and DJ Harvey. This club was created by the company that founded Yellow, a legendary club in Nishi-Azabu. You need to register online before being admitted.

388 **WWW**
AT: RISE BUILDING
13-17 Udagawacho
Shibuya-ku ①
+81 (0)3-5458-7685
www-shibuya.jp

This building used to be a cinema, which is why it has a multi-level floor. There is always something exciting going on, whether a gig by a young Japanese indie band or a performance by world-renowned jazz musicians. They also invite DJs and small theatre groups sometimes.

389 **SOUP**

AT: MIKASA BUILDING
**3-9-10 Kami-Ochiai
Shinjuku-ku** ⑫
+81 (0)3-6909-3000
ochiaisoup.com

Located in the basement of a bath house in a quiet residential area. This place only admits 100 people so the atmosphere is friendly. Do look for the bath house and launderette, and go down the stairs of the same building.

390 **AOYAMA HACHI**

AT: AOYAMA BUILDING,
2ND-4TH FL.
**4-5-9 Shibuya
Shibuya-ku** ①
+81 (0)3-5766-4887
aoyama-hachi.net

They have three DJ floors and a lounge bar on the fourth floor with a nice selection of music events including house and techno as well as soul, jazz, and reggae. The stylish atmosphere and excellent sound system attract huge crowds and world-famous DJs.

25 THINGS TO DO
WITH CHILDREN

———————

5

PARKS

that charge no admission

---

391 RINSHI NO MORI PARK
5-chome, Shimo-Meguro
Meguro-ku ⑭
+81 (0)3-3792-3800
tokyo-park.or.jp

This park was used as an experimental forestry station until the late seventies and reopened as a park in 1989. This explains why there are so many trees including rare trees, like the handkerchief tree, and rare plants, such as the native dandelion called *Kanto tampopo*.

392 TODOROKI KEIKOKU PARK
1-22, 2-37/38 Todoroki
Setagaya-ku ⑬

This park was designated a site of scenic beauty by Tokyo's Metropolitan Government. It is just a short walk from the nearest station, Todoroki. As you walk down the trail, you will forget that you are in busy Tokyo.

393 SAKURAZAKA PARK
Roppongi Hills
Roppongi
Minato-ku ⑥
roppongihills.com

This park is also known as 'Robo Robo Koen' as you can run into robots, which were created by the Korean artist Choi Jeonghwa, here and there. The park is best known for its tower of 44 robots and its slides. Don't look any further if your kids love to play.

394 TONERI IKIKI PARK

6-3-1 Toneri
Adachi-ku

Many of the features in this park were inspired by Japanese folk tales. The slope features a red demon and kids come out of the demon's mouth – very interesting. It is rather a small park, but it has a lot of stories (literally) and unique.

395 KINUTA PARK

1-1 Kinuta Koen
Setagaya-ku ⑬

There is an art museum, a bird sanctuary, and an athletics facility on site. This family park also has nice lawns with cherry trees. An excellent place for a picnic perhaps?

392 TODOROKI KEIKOKU PARK

5 nice
ZOOS and AQUARIUMS

396 INOKASHIRA PARK ZOO

1-17-6 Gotenyama
Musashino-shi
+81 (0)422-46-1100
tokyo-zoo.net/zoo/ino/

Inokashira Park Zoo occupies approximately one third of Inokashira Park. This zoo is home to over 200 species, some of which are not kept in cages but in enclosures, like the squirrels. The park also has a duck sanctuary and breeds mandarin ducks which it releases into the wild.

397 UENO ZOOLOGICAL GARDENS

9-83 Ueno Koen
Taito-ku ⑩
+81(0)3-3828-5171
tokyo-zoo.net/zoo/ueno

Japan's oldest zoo opened in 1882 and attracts more than 3.000.000 visitors annually, who come to see 500 species of animals including a giant panda. Each animal is kept in an enclosure that replicates the environment they would usually live in. Ducks and sea gulls like to stop in the natural pond.

398 SHINAGAWA AQUARIUM

3-2-1 Katsushima
Shinagawa-ku ⑭
+81 (0)3-3762-3433
aquarium.gr.jp

One of the popular features of this aquarium is a tunnel tank that simulates the environment of Tokyo Bay. You will be amazed by how many creatures actually populate the bay. Enjoy a 360-degree panoramic view of the seals as they swim through the tank tunnel.

399 SUNSHINE AQUARIUM

3-1-1 Higashi-Ikebukuro
Toshima-ku ⑪
+81 (0)3-3989-3466
sunshinecity.co.jp/
aquarium

This bright and airy aquarium is actually located on the building's rooftop. Here you can see penguins swim overhead and get close to several water animals. Check the feeding times for the penguins, pelicans, seals, and other animals.

400 SUMIDA AQUARIUM

1-1-2 Oshiage
Sumida-ku ⑮
+81 (0)3-5619-1821
sumida-aquarium.com

This aquarium is located on the fifth and sixth floors of Tokyo Solamachi. See beautiful goldfish swim in the Edorium, including 'ordinary' goldfish (*ryukin* and *wakin*) as well as roundfish (*ranchu*). Take a look behind the scenes and learn more about the keepers' jobs in the Aqua Lab.

397 UENO ZOOLOGICAL GARDENS

5 great children's
BOOKSHOPS

---

401 CRAYON HOUSE

3-8-15 Kita-Aoyama
Minato-ku ③
+81 (0)3-3406-6308
crayonhouse.co.jp

This bookshop was established by the writer Keiko Ochiai in 1976 to promote culture from the viewpoint of children and women. In addition to books, they also sell toys, organic cosmetics and vegetables. Don't forget to try the homemade cakes in the onsite organic restaurant.

402 BOOKS KYOBUNKWAN

4-5-1 Ginza
Chuo-ku ⑧
+81 (0)3-3561-8446
kyobunkwan.co.jp

This bookshop opened 120 years ago. In 1998, they added a children's section, called Narnia. The shop offers a range of around 15.000 titles, including popular older books and recent publications. They organise panel discussions and events. A cosy place for small children.

403 EHON HOUSE

1-7-14 Mejiro
Toshima-ku ⑪
+81 (0)3-3985-3350
ehon-house.co.jp

This shop sells imported picture books, mainly from European countries, including Germany, France, Italy, the Netherlands, and Sweden as well as English language learning materials for children. They also have a range of products inspired by children's books, like Moomin and Pippi Longstocking.

404 CHIE NO KI NO MI

2-3-14 Ebisu-Nishi
Shibuya-ku ②
+81 (0)3-5428-4611
chienokinomi-books.jp

The idea behind this bookshop's range is that parents want their children to read and love books. In addition to books, they also sell wooden toys that are child-proof. Parents and children can read together in the reading area on the second floor.

405 MIWA SHOBO

2-3 Kanda Jinbocho
Chiyoda-ku ⑨
+81 (0)3-3261-2348
miwa-shobo.com
childbook@miwa-shobo.com

This secondhand bookshop specialises in children's books. They have a wide range of picture books and children's literature, from Japan and other countries. They also sell a range of children's magazines from the 1950s and colouring books.

401 CRAYON HOUSE

5 places for kids on
A RAINY DAY

---

406 TOKYO TOY MUSEUM
4-20 Yotsuya
Shinjuku-ku ⑦
+81 (0)3-5367-9601
goodtoy.org/ttm

This museum exhibits over 5000 toys from Japan and other countries in ten classrooms of a former primary school and is great fun for small children. They also have 10.000 toys that you and your kids can play with and a shop where you can buy gifts for children of all ages.

407 INTERNATIONAL LIBRARY OF CHILDREN'S LITERATURE
12-49 Ueno Koen
Taito-ku ⑩
+81 (0)3-3827-2053
kodomo.go.jp

One of the National Diet Libraries, which has a collection of over 10.000 children's books including 1800 titles in foreign languages. Learn more about the history of children's literature and picture books after the Meiji period in the second-floor gallery. The building, which was designed by Tadao Ando, is worth a visit.

408 SONY EXPLORASCIENCE
AT: AQUA CITY ODAIBA, 5TH FL.
1-7-1 Daiba
Minato-ku ⑮
+81 (0)3-5531-2186
sonyexplorascience.jp

A science museum where you can learn more about Sony's latest technology for electronics and games. The exhibition is divided into four zones and one studio. Transform into different characters using AR Technology in the Information & Entertainment Zone.

409 MIRAIKAN
THE NATIONAL MUSEUM OF
EMERGING SCIENCE AND
INNOVATION
2-3-6 Aomi
Koto-ku ⑮
+81 (0)3-3570-9151
miraikan.jst.go.jp

A great place to learn all there is to know about cutting-edge science and technology, with plenty of interactive displays. Even more enjoyable if you download the official app to your smartphone. On Saturdays, they don't charge admission for anyone under 18 (does not include the temporary exhibitions).

410 SANRIO PUROLAND
1-31 Ochiai
Tama-shi
+81 (0)42-339-1111
puroland.jp

An amusement park where you can meet the characters Sanrio created, such as Hello Kitty and My Melody. And what's more, you don't have to worry about the weather as this is an indoor park. Some of the merchandise they sell can only be bought here. If you are celebrating a birthday or another anniversary, you'll be treated to a bunch of fun specials.

5 SHOPS and
SHOPPING CENTRES
where kids can spend hours

---

411 HAKUHINKAN TOY PARK

8-8-11 Ginza
Chuo-ku ⑧
+81 (0)3-3571-8008
hakuhinkan.co.jp

This place is the stuff that kids' dreams are made of, selling everything from Barbie dolls to video games, on five floors. Check out the Hakuhinkan Racing Park on the fourth floor, where you can play with remote controlled cars. You may have to jostle for space with some grown-up kids though.

412 YAMASHIROYA

6-14-6 Ueno
Taito-ku ⑩
+81 (0)3-3831-2320
e-yamashiroya.com

This popular toy store in Ueno has been here forever and sells various toys and party staples on six floors. Look out for their collectors' items, such as soft vinyl figures from classic TV series. Open until 9.30 pm.

413 AQUA CITY ODAIBA

1-7-1 Daiba
Minato-ku ⑮
+81 (0)3-3599-4700
aquacity.jp

Aqua City is a large 'entertainment shopping mall'. Here you'll find a toy shop and a 100 yen store, as well as Tokyo Leisure Land where you can take *purikura* and a shop where you can buy capsule toys. It also provides a place for children to nap.

414 TOKYO CHARACTER STREET
AT: FIRST AVENUE TOKYO STATION

1-9-1 Marunouchi ⑧
Chiyoda-ku
+81 (0)3-3210-0077
tokyoeki-1bangai.co.jp

In the underground shopping center in Tokyo Station. The street is lined with shops of popular characters, including Hello Kitty, Rirakkuma, and Ultraman as well as the official shops of Tokyo's TV stations. They even have a shop where you can buy capsule toys from 100 vending machines.

415 TOKYO DOME CITY

1-3-61 Koraku
Bunkyo-ku ⑩
+81 (0)3-3817-6001
tokyo-dome.co.jp

A baseball stadium, amusement park, spa, restaurants, and a hotel in one location. ASOBono! is Tokyo's largest indoor facility and a great place for kids to use their imagination while playing.

414 TOKYO CHARACTER STREET

HOTEL CHINZANSO TOKYO

20 PLACES
TO SLEEP

─────────

5

AFFORDABLE

accommodations

---

416 HOTEL VILLA FONTAINE TOKYO-KUDANSHITA

2-4-4 Nishi-Kanda
Chiyoda-ku ⑨
+81 (0)3-3222-8880
hvf.jp/kudanshita

Villa Fontaine is a budget hotel chain. Many people rely on this chain when travelling for business, as all their hotels are located in very convenient areas. The one near the Imperial Palace is an excellent choice for anyone who also wants to do some sightseeing in Tokyo. Each room is well-equipped.

417 TOKYO GREEN PALACE

2 Nibancho
Chiyoda-ku ⑤
+81 (0)3-5210-4600
tokyogp.com

This hotel is bright and clean and delivers good service at an affordable price. The breakfast buffet changes every morning so people can enjoy it even if they stay at the hotel for several days on end. They serve a lunch buffet on the weekends as well.

418 CENTURION HOTEL CABIN TOWER

3-12-3 Akasaka
Minato-ku ⑤
+81 (0)3-6229-6336
centurion-hotel.com/
residential/cabin_rooms

If you wish to stay in the centre but are travelling on a shoestring, this hotel could be an option for you. Basically this is a designer's hostel. What the cabins (yes, the word cabin is more suited here) lack, i.e., space, they make up for this in terms of practicality and style.

419 **THE PRIME POD GINZA**
AT: GINZA DUPLEX TOWER
5/13 BUILDING, 13TH FL.
5-13 Ginza
Chuo-ku ⑧
+81 (0)3-5550-0147
theprimepod.jp/ginza

Located in the expensive district of Ginza. Each pod (here each compartment is called a 'pod,' not a 'cabin') has a 19-inch flat screen and a safe. The Serta mattress makes your stay very comfortable. A launderette is available, and you can enjoy coffee made with freshly-ground beans.

420 **NINE HOURS**
AT: NINE HOURS SHINJUKU –
NORTH BUILDING, 3RD-8TH FL.
1-4-15 Hyakunincho
Shinjuku-ku ⑦
+81 (0)3-5291-7337
ninehours.co.jp

This stylish capsule hotel is all about comfort, providing towels, slippers, a toothbrush, something comfy to lounge in. You can eat (as you are not allowed to take food in your capsule) and work (printers and faxes available) in the lounge on the eighth floor.

5
LUXURIOUS
hotels

---

421 HOSHINOYA TOKYO
1-9-1 Otemachi
Chiyoda-ku ⑧
+81 (0)3-6214-5151
hoshinoyatokyo.com

A luxury *ryokan* (Japanese inn) that offers you an extraordinary experience, just a 10-minute walk from Tokyo Station. The building is surrounded by several skyscrapers, and this contrast makes the hotel even more extraordinary. There is an open-air hot spring only for guests.

422 HOTEL RYUMEIKAN OCHANOMIZU HONTEN
3-4 Kanda-Surugadai
Chiyoda-ku ⑨
+81 (0)3-3251-1135
ryumeikan-honten.jp

Ryumeikan has been around for many years as a *ryokan* and was renovated and updated to a more contemporary style in 2014. The guest rooms resemble a countryside *ryokan* but here you get to sleep on a comfortable bed instead of on a futon. Enjoy a soothing bath in their bathtub made of Shigaraki ware. You won't get to experience this anywhere else.

423 HOTEL CHINZANSO TOKYO
2-10-8 Sekiguchi
Bunkyo-ku ⑪
+81 (0)3-3493-1111
hotel-chinzanso-tokyo.jp

Chinzan literally translates as a 'mountain of camellias' as this place used to be a beauty spot where wild camellias grew. The hotel opened in 1992 on the site of the Chinzanso wedding centre. Guests can enjoy its gorgeous garden throughout the year.

424 IMPERIAL HOTEL

1-1-1 Uchisaiwaicho
Chiyoda-ku ⑧
+81 (0)3-3504-1111
imperialhotel.co.jp

The hotel is as Japanese as it gets. Opened in 1890, this was the first hotel to offer a laundry service and buffet-style restaurant in Japan. In Japan, an all-you-can-eat buffet is often called *baikingu*, or Viking. The president of the hotel at that time was inspired to call it like that by a scene in the film *The Vikings*, in which a band of Vikings attack their food with gusto.

425 THE PENINSULA TOKYO

1-8-1 Yurakucho
Chiyoda-ku ⑧
+81 (0)3-6270-2888
tokyo.peninsula.com

Needless to say, this hotel belongs to the chain of Peninsula Hotels. Since its opening in 2007, the hotel has received five stars in the Forbes ranking and several other awards. The guest rooms are decorated with natural wood in a distinctive Japanese style. The restaurants facing the Imperial Palace are an excellent choice for lunch.

423 HOTEL CHINZANSO TOKYO

5 of the best
BOUTIQUE
hotels

---

426 TRUNK (HOTEL)

5-31 Jingumae
Shibuya-ku ③
+81 (0)3-5766-3210
trunk-hotel.com

Opened in 2017, and located between Shibuya and Harajuku, this hotel inspired a new trend in Japan's hotel industry. This is not just a hotel. Calling itself a 'hotel for socialising', it has a bar lounge and restaurants where you can do just that.

427 HOTEL CLASKA

1-3-18 Chuocho
Meguro-ku ⑭
+81 (03)-3719-8121
claska.com/hotel/index.
html

This hotel is located on the fourth through the seventh floors of of the Claska complex. The rooms were all designed by contemporary architects and artists who are representative of today's Japan. There are four types of rooms: Modern, Tatami, Contemporary, and DIY. In Tatami rooms, you can enjoy a good combination of Japanese tradition and modern style.

428 LYURO TOKYO KIYOSUMI

1-1-7 Kiyosumi
Koto-ku ⑮
+81 (0)3-6458-5540
thesharehotels.com/lyuro

This hotel also opened in 2017 in Kiyosumi Shirakawa. This area has popped up on everyone's radar because of the many organic cafes and restaurants that opened here in recent years. Some of the rooms have a 'River View bath', where you can enjoy a relaxing time gazing at the Sumida River.

429 WIRED HOTEL

2-16-2 Asakusa
Taito-ku ⑩
+81 (0)3-5830-7931
wiredhotel.com

Another 'wabi-sabi modern' hotel that opened in 2017. They have several types of rooms, including a dorm-style room and more luxuriously appointed ones. All the rooms, including the dormitory, have been kitted out with Swedish top-quality brand Duxiana beds. In the cafe and bar Zakbaran, you can sample healthy desserts made with tofu.

430 HOTEL S

1-11-6 Nishi-Azabu
Minato-ku ⑥
+81 (0)3-5771-2469
hr-roppongi.jp/hotelS

Located between Roppongi Hills and the Nishi-Azabu crossing, this hotel is convenient for anyone interested in a taste of Tokyo's nightlife. Some of the rooms have organic soaps and other amenities that female guests will appreciate. There are 12 apartments designated for those who plan to stay for more than a month.

428 LYURO TOKYO KIYOSUMI

5 hotels that serve an
EXCELLENT BREAKFAST

---

431 THE AGNES HOTEL & APARTMENTS TOKYO
2-20-1 Kagurazaka
Shinjuku-ku ⑤
+81 (0)3-3267-5505
agneshotel.com

The Agnes Hotel is located off the main street, and consequently only those in the know stay there. On weekdays, non-guests can also enjoy the hotel's breakfast buffet. Start your day with a glass of freshly-squeezed orange juice. Eggs are cooked to order.

432 PALACE HOTEL
1-1-1 Marunouchi
Chiyoda-ku ⑧
+81 (0)3-3211-5211
palacehoteltokyo.com

Grand Kitchen on the ground floor serves breakfast for guests and non-guests on weekdays. Take your pick from the buffet 'Grand Kitchen Breakfast' or choose the 'Palace Morning' option that lets you add dishes to your breakfast buffet, such as egg benedict or pot-au-feu.

433 TOKYO STATION HOTEL
1-9-1 Marunouchi
Chiyoda-ku ⑧
+81 (0)3-5220-1111
tokyostationhotel.jp

As its name suggests, Tokyo Station Hotel is located in Tokyo Station. The Atrium guest lounge is located on the top floor and serves a breakfast buffet with 110 different dishes. Only for hotel guests, however, so why don't you consider spending a night at the hotel if you have a good appetite?

434 HILLTOP HOTEL

1-1 Kanda-Surugadai
Chiyoda-ku ⑨
+81 (0)3-3293-2311
yamanoue-hotel.co.jp

Many authors, such as Yukiko Mishima and Yashinari Kawabata, loved this hotel. They still serve the breakfast of choice of these authors. You can choose between a Japanese or western-style breakfast. The first one includes grilled fish, a Japanese omelette, seaweed, pickled plums, miso soup, porridge and more. Both options are a well-balanced way to start your day.

435 HOTEL NIWA TOKYO

1-1-16 Kanda Misakicho
Chiyoda-ku ⑨
+81 (0)3-3293-0028
hotelniwa.jp

This modern hotel with a distinctive Japanese twist serves a breakfast buffet. Its salad bar has a selection of over 20 different fresh vegetables, which it sources directly from contract farms. Egg dishes are cooked to order. You can also enjoy a seasonal vegetable soup, and a bowl of rice and miso soup.

WAKASU KAIHIN PARK

45 WEEKEND ACTIVITIES

5 destinations for
A ONE-DAY TRIP FROM TOKYO

---

436 HAKONE
Kanagawa

The trip from from Shinjuku to Hakone by Odakyu Romance Car takes roughly 90 minutes. Hakone is known for its hot springs, but there are also several museums worth visiting. At Honma Yoseki Museum, you can observe how the craftsmen make beautiful wooden crafts called *Yoseki zukuri*.

437 SAKURA
Chiba

Just one hour from Tokyo Station and 30 minutes from Narita Airport, Sakura City is a residential suburb of Tokyo. It looks quite different from the capital however. Prepare to be amazed by the samurai's residences from the Edo period. Cycling around Inba Swamp can be fun.

438 HITACHINAKA
Ibaraki

Hitachinaka has a 200-hectare national park called Hitachi Kaihin Koen (aka Hitachi Seaside Park). The park is known for its flower gardens, attracting people all year round, even in winter! There are a few historical spots, including Hiraisho Hakuaso, a Mesozoic Cretaceous formation where you can find ammonites.

439 MISHIMA
Shizuoka

This city is located on the road to Mount Fuji from Tokyo. As the weather tends to be sunny here in winter, you may be able to admire beautiful snow-capped Mount Fuji. In May, you may spot fireflies in the area within walking distance of JR Station.

440 MATSUMOTO
Nagano

The perfect place for soba noodle lovers. Nagawa area, in Matsumoto, is known for its buckwheat and even has its own native variety. One of the main sightseeing spots is Nakamachi area, just a 10-minute walk from Matsumoto Station, with its typical black and white warehouses. Don't forget to visit Matsumoto Castle, which is a national treasure.

5

WEEKEND ESCAPES

---

441 CHICHIBU
Saitama

A good area for trekking. Mitsumine Shrine at the top of the mountain is considered to be one of the most sacred places in Japan. There is a natural hot spring and plenty of accommodation. After bathing, enjoy a cup of coffee brewed with spring water.

442 TATEYAMA
Chiba

Located in the south of Boso Peninsula, Chiba Prefecture, the trip here takes approximately two hours from Tokyo by express train. There are several beautiful beaches, that are especially popular in summertime. With seafood in abundance, this is a good place to enjoy excellent quality sushi.

443 IZU
Shizuoka

Hop on a bullet train at Tokyo station, and you will arrive in Izu after just 45 minutes. The climate here is a moderate one. There are many hot springs in the area, and some of them are run like a public bath house: you can use them after paying a small fee.

444 NIKKO
Tochigi

Many people take a day trip to Nikko but there is loads more to see there. Canoe down the Kinugawa River and on Chuzenji Lake and go fishing in the Ojika River. You can stay at a *ryokan* with a hot spring.

445 FUJI KAWAGUCHIKO
Yamanashi

Four of Fuji's five lakes (Fuji Goko) are situated in Fuji Kawaguchiko. A place where you are guaranteed to have gorgeous views of Mount Fuji, in other words. Cherry blossoms in spring, lavender in summer, bright red foliage in autumn, and snow in winter… enjoy nature's splendour here throughout the seasons.

5 nice

RUNNING

trails

---

446 **KOMAZAWA OLYMPIC PARK**
1-1 Komazawa Koen
Setagaya-ku ⑬
+81 (0)3-3421-6431
tef.or.jp/kopgp

The 2,1-kilometre-long trail winds its way around the park, without traffic lights. It is more or less flat, and you can run while enjoying views of the park which change depending on the season. Near the park, there are a few facilities that let runners use their locker room.

447 **MEIJI JINGU GAIEN**
1-1 Kasumigaokamachi
Shinjuku-ku ④
+81 (0)3-3401-0312
meijijingugaien.jp

The road around Jingu Gaien is 1,3 kilometres long, but include Akasaka Imperial Gardens for a 3,3-kilometre run. There are a few shower facilities around the trail. One of them is a public bath house called Shimizu-yu (3-12-3 Minami-Aoyama, Minato-ku) which has towels and shampoo.

448 **MEGURO RIVER**
Nakameguro
Meguro-ku ②

A five-kilometre trail. The river is a popular spot for cherry blossom viewing from late March to early April. Runners are welcomed at the Kohmeisen public bath house (1-6-1 Kami-Meguro, Meguro-ku). There is even an open-air bath on the rooftop.

449 ODAIBA KAIHIN PARK
1-4 Daiba
Minato-ku ⑮
+81 (0)3-5500-2455

There are two trails in the park, of five and seven kilometres respectively. Both have a sea view, and are flat with no traffic lights, making this a perfect option for beginners. You can use the locker room and showers at Marine House near the start of the trail.

450 SHAKUJII PARK
1-26-1 Shakujiidai
Nerima-ku
+81 (0)3-3996-3950

The park has a 1,75-kilometre trail around Shakujii Pond. Unfortunately, there are no shower facilities in the park but you can use the coin-operated lockers at Shakujii Park Furusato Bunkakan next to the park. Though beautiful Sanpoji Pond (there are two ponds in the park) is not on the trail, it is definitely worth visiting.

449 ODAIBA KAIHIN PARK

5

PUBLIC SWIMMING POOLS

451 **TOKYO METROPOLITAN GYMNASIUM**
1-17-1 Sendagaya
Shibuya-ku ④
+81 (0)3-5474-2114
tef.or.jp/kopgp

Tokyo Metropolitan Gymnasium, which opened in 1956, was the main venue for the 1964 Tokyo Olympic Games. There are two swimming pools: 50 metres and 25 metres. Bring your favourite shampoo and soap, as they are not provided. If you buy a one-day ticket, you can also use the training room and the exercise studio.

452 **HAGINAKA PARK SWIMMING POOL**
3-26-46 Haginaka
Ota-ku ⑭
+81 (0)3-3743-2155
haginaka.kbm.cc

This swimming centre, run by Ota City, has six pools. The outdoor pools are open from mid-July to the end of August, but the indoor pools are available throughout the year. From September to June, the pools are heated. There are indoor and outdoor water slides, so kids are bound to love this pool.

453 **TOKYO TATSUMI** INTERNATIONAL SWIMMING CENTER
2-8-10 Tatsumi
Koto-ku ⑮
+81 (0)3-5569-5061
tatsumi-swim.net

This 50-metre swimming pool is used for official competitions but is also open to people who enjoy a good swim, including children. On the days when there are no competitions, you can use the pool all day for a fixed price.

454 SUMIDA SPORTS KENKO CENTER

1-6-1 Higashi-Sumida
Sumida-ku ⑮
+81 (0)3-5247-7755
sumispo.com

Who cares about the weather when you can enjoy this fantastic indoor pool. There are five areas: a pool for infants and toddlers, a pool for children, a flowing pool, a 25-metre pool, and a water slide. On the 25th of every month, admission is free. Natural light flows into this indoor pool, making it a perfect place for a swim.

455 EAST CHOFU PARK POOL

5-13-1 Minami-Yukigaya
Ota-ku ⑭
+81 (0)3-3728-7651
east-chofu.jp

Another swimming pool run by Ota City. The 25-metre indoor pool is open until 9 pm, but you can spend as much time as you want here. The outdoor pools are available in July and August. The 50-metre outdoor pool is usually less crowded than the other areas.

451 TOKYO METROPOLITAN GYMNASIUM

5
HIKING / TREKKING
trails

---

456 TAMA KYURYO
Hachioji-shi/Hino-shi/
Tama-shi/Inagi-shi/
Machida-shi

Tama Kyuryo is a vast area, extending from the border with Kanagawa Prefecture to the foot of Mount Takao. There are over 20 hiking trails in the area. One of the trails will lead you to the Sakuragaoka Rotary that was featured in Studio Ghibli's film *Whisper of the Heart.*

457 MOUNT JINBA
Hachioji-shi

This mountain (altitude: 857 metres) is located along the border of Hachioji City, Tokyo and Sagamihara City, Kanagawa. It is not difficult to climb, even for beginners. At the end of April, the mountain ridge is covered with cherry blossoms.

458 MOUNT ODAKE
Nishitama-gun

With an altitude of 1266 metres Mount Odake is one of the 200 highest mountains in Japan, where there are over 10.000 mountains. If you are not an advanced hiker, then use the cable car service. There are several hot springs around the mountain, don't forget to stop for a bath after your hike.

459 MOUNT TAKAMIZU
Ome-shi

This hiking trail winds its way along the ridge of three mountains: Takamizu (759 m), Iwatake Ishiyama (793 m), and Sogaku (756 m). It takes approximately four hours to walk the entire trail, making it suitable for beginners, including first-timers and primary school children.

460 MOUNT KAGENOBU
Hachioji-shi

This mountain is located between Mount Takao and Jinba. There are two traditional style tearooms (*chaya*) where you can enjoy beautiful views of Mount Fuji at the summit. If you take a bus from Takao Station and get off at Kobotoke, it takes about an hour to get to the summit.

5
CYCLING
trails

---

461 EDOGAWA CYCLING ROAD
BY THE EDOGAWA RIVER
Edogawa-ku
edogawacr.com

A 60-kilometre trail from the inlet of the Edo River to the point where it splits from the Tone River. Most of the trail is paved, so it is relatively easy for everyone. Please note the road is not for cyclists only, meaning you must always make way for pedestrians.

462 WAKASU SEASIDE PARK
3-1-2 Wakasu
Koto-ku ⑮
+81 (0)3-3522-3225
tptc.co.jp/en/c_park/03_07

This six-kilometre trail along Tokyo Bay is almost flat, making it the ideal course if you want to bike with your children. Rental bikes (26 inches and 20 inches) and tandem bikes are available. They also have animal-shaped bicycles and tricycles for children.

463 YOYOGI CYCLING CENTRE
2-1 Yoyogi Kamizonocho
Shibuya-ku ⑦
+81 (0)3-3465-6855

Yoyogi Cycling Centre is located in Yoyogi Park. You can rent bicycles for adults and children as well as tandem bikes for two. There is an area where children can practise riding bikes with training wheels.

464 **TAMAGAWA CYCLING ROAD**
BY THE TAMA RIVER
Ota-ku ⑭

A 60-kilometre scenic trail along the Tama River. If you want to enjoy great views while cycling, this is a good choice. The trail runs past residential areas and public transport stations, so you can easily find toilets, vending machines, and convenience stores.

465 **SHOWA MEMORIAL PARK**
3173 Midoricho
Tachikawa-shi
showakinen-koen.jp

This park has a 14-kilometre cycling trail, and three 'cycling centres' where you can rent a bike. You can choose from 18 to 26-inches or rent a tandem bike. And naturally, you can also bring your own. This course is for cyclists only, no pedestrians allowed.

462 **WAKASU SEASIDE PARK**

5
ROCK-CLIMBING
spots

---

466 **ROCKY BOULDERING GYM**

5-4-38 Konan
Minato-ku ⑭
+81 (0)3-6712-9538
rockyclimbing.com

The largest rock-climbing studio in Tokyo, which can accommodate up to 160 people. They have several courses that people of all levels can enjoy. Booking is not essential. Make sure to wear comfortable clothes for climbing and a pair of socks. You can also rent rock-climbing shoes.

467 **BOULDER VILLAGE**

1-8-4 Nihonbashi-
Bakurocho
Chuo-ku ⑮
+81 (0)3-6661-7990
boulder-village.com

This rock-climbing gym is located in the business district and is open until 11 pm. There are 'problems', developed by professional climbers, depending on the level. Each level is indicated in a different colour. If you start from the yellow hold marked with an 'S' (as in Start) for example, then just follow the yellow stickers up the wall.

468 **ENERGY CLIMBING GYM**

4-9-9 Takadanobaba
Shinjuku-ku ⑪
+81 (0)3-6279-3155
7a.biglobe.ne.jp/~energy

This gym is just a one-minute walk from Takadanobaba station. The main climbing area has a polytope wall and a 130-degree slope for advanced climbers. There is also a beginners' area. A half-hour trial course is available.

469 BOULDERING GYM GRANNY

6-7-3 Higashi-Ueno
Taito-ku ⑩
+81 (0)3-6874-8112
granny-ueno.jp

There are four walls with a 90-, 115-, 125-, and 170-degree angle respectively. The staff members create new problems every day, so you can try different courses no matter how many times you go. If you are a group of four or more, it may be a good idea to call them before you go to check availability.

470 LAGO

1-7-3 Honan
Suginami-ku
+81 (0)3-6676-6012
lakers.co.jp/lago/index.html

This gym can be used by six-year-olds or over. Up to 2 pm on weekdays, women and children can enjoy climbing for just 600 yen. This is a good choice if you and your kids want to give rock-climbing a try. Free lessons available for first-timers.

5
FISHING
spots

---

471 BENKEI FISHING CLUB
4-26 Kioicho
Chiyoda-ku ⑤
+81 (0)3-3238-0012
maidokun.com/
benkeifishing/

Did you know that you can go bass fishing in Akasaka area? Fish from Benkei Bridge or hire a flyboat. There are carp and snakehead, and in winter, you might even pull up a rainbow trout. You can book a boat online for the weekends.

472 ICHIGAYA FISH CENTER
1-1 Ichigaya Tamachi
Shinjuku-ku ⑤
+81 (0)3-3260-1324
ichigaya-fc.com/fishing/

Tsuribori is a leisure spot where you can enjoy fishing in an artificial pond. This *tsuribori* is located near Icjigaya Station, in the heart of Tokyo, where many people enjoy fishing for carp. There is a 'mini fishing' area, where small children can fish for goldfish and small carp.

473 KASAI RINKAI PARK
6-2-1 Rinkaicho
Edogawa-ku
+81 (0)3-5696-1331

There are a few fishing spots in this park, which faces Tokyo Bay. You can fish for gobies and bass throughout the year and some other fish depending on the season. Please note that surfcasting is not allowed here and there are plenty of stingrays, which have a venomeous sting of course.

474 THE EBITORI RIVER

6-chome Haneda
Ota-ku ⑭

The Ebitori River is a class A river near Haneda Airport. The name translates as 'prawn catching river' but you also catch gobies and young sea bass here. Bring your rod and other tackle as there is no shop nearby and a packed lunch if necessary.

475 YUMENOSHIMA GREEN PARK

1, 2, 3-chome
Yumenoshima
Koto-ku ⑮
+81-(0)3-5569-8672
tptc.co.jp/park/03_03

In this park, which is only a three-minute walk from the nearest station, you can fish spiny gobies and bass and for free. There is a fence on the bank, so you can let your kids fish with no worries.

471 BENKEI FISHING CLUB

5

FOOD FESTIVALS

476 AOYAMA PAIN FESTIVAL
AT: UNU FARMER'S MARKET
5-53-70 Jingumae
Shibuya-ku ③
bread-lab.com

The most popular event at the UNU Farmer's Market. This festival lasts a weekend with more than 60 bakeries from all over the country participating every day. Some bakeries sell special sandwiches that were created just for this festival.

477 SHIMOKITAZAWA CURRY FESTIVAL
AROUND SHIMOKITAZAWA STATION
Setagaya-ku ⑫
curryfes.pw

Shimokitazawa is known for its small theatres, but it also has a few unique curry shops. At the festival, you can enjoy a 'curry stroll' from Indian and Thai curry to curry-flavoured *karaage* (fried chicken) and *omuraisu* (rice wrapped in a thin omelette), collect stamps each time you eat to get the limited edition T-shirt at the end of your stroll.

478 THAI FESTIVAL
YOYOGI PARK
2-1 Yoyogi Kamizonocho
Shibuya-ku ③
thaifestival.jp

This festival is organised by the Thai Embassy. With over 300.000 attendees every year, this is the most popular event in Yoyogi Park. From *tom yum goong* to *khao soi*, you can taste authentic Thai dishes as well as popular tropical fruit from Thailand.

479 **TOKYO RAMEN SHOW**
KOMAZAWA OLYMPIC PARK
1-1 Komazawa Koen
+81 (0)3-3490-3810
Setagaya-ku ⑬
ramenshow.com

The largest outdoor ramen event in Japan was first organised in 2009. You can taste regional-style ramen from all over the country here as well as all kinds of ramen soups – *Shio* (salt-based), *Shoyu* (soy-sauce based), *Miso*, *Paitan* (white broth) and *Tonkotsu* (broth made with pork bones) – with a variety of toppings.

480 **OKINAWA MATSURI**
AT: YOYOGI PARK
2-1 Yoyogi Kamizonocho
Shibuya-ku ③
okifes.tokyo

This festival promotes Okinawa, not just its food but also its music and traditional culture. Enjoy *goya champuru* (stir-fried bitter melon) and *mimiga* (pig's ear) while drinking an Orion Beer, and dance to *eisa* with friendly Okinawan people.

HACHIKO STATUE

20 RANDOM FACTS AND USEFUL DETAILS

5 things you should
NOT DO
in Japan

---

481 WEAR SHOES INSIDE THE HOUSE

You should take off your shoes before entering someone's house, a *ryokan*, or a temple's main hall unless you are told that it is not necessary. If there are slippers available, you should wear them instead. When visiting a temple in winter, take an extra pair of socks to ensure your feet stay warm.

482 BLOW YOUR NOSE LOUDLY

People in Japan don't like making noises except when they are eating noodles. If you need to blow your nose, use a paper tissue and both hands so you can do it quietly. In Japan, people do not use handkerchiefs to blow their nose.

483 KISS ON THE TRAIN, IN THE STREETS, IN A RESTAURANT, ETC.

Even if you wish to express your affection to your loved one who is sitting right beside you, don't kiss them in public. This is just not done in Japanese culture (though you may come across kissing couples later in the evening).

484 PLAY WITH CHOPSTICKS

There is such a thing as chopstick etiquette. Sticking chopsticks in a bowl of rice and passing food from chopsticks to chopsticks may be acceptable for non-Japanese people but Japanese people associate this type of behavior with funeral rites.

485 WASH YOUR BODY IN THE BATHTUB

If you go to a public bathing house or communal baths in a *ryokan*, you must wash your body before diving into the bathtub. Do not dip your towel or face flannel in the water. These rules are for hygiene purposes. You also prefer clean water in your bath, don't you?

5

POPULAR
MEETING SPOTS

486 HACHIKO STATUE
OUTSIDE SHIBUYA STATION
(JR, TOKYO METRO)
1-2 Dogenzaka
Shibuya-ku ①

This is the statue of a legendary dog who was so loyal to his master that he used to wait for his master to come home in front of Shibuya Station even after he died. You might have seen Hachi in the film *Hachi: A Dog's Tale*, which was inspired by this dog's tale.

487 MOYAI STATUE
AT: SOUTH GATE SHIBUYA
STATION (JR, TOKYO METRO)
1-1 Dogenzaka
Shibuya-ku ①

While this may remind you of the statues on Easter Island, this statue comes from the Isle of Niijima which is a part of Tokyo. The name 'Moyai' comes from *moyau*, which is the island's dialect and means 'to cooperate'. The statues on the island were created about 50 years ago.

488 GIN NO SUZU SQUARE / SILVER BELL
Tokyo Station, Underground central passage
Chiyoda-ku ⑧

This is supposed to be one of the popular meeting places at Tokyo Station, but you may find it very difficult to find as there are so many shops inside the station. Download the East Japan Railway app to your smartphone so you won't get lost.

489 SHINJUKU NO ME / THE EYE OF SHINJUKU

AT: SUBARU BUILDING

1-7-2 Nishi-Shinjuku
Shinjuku-ku ⑦

Shinjuku no Me, also known as *L'Oeil de Shinjuku* (The Eye of Shinkjuku) is an acrylic object created by a female sculptor called Yoshiko Miyashita in 1969. This work, measuring 10 metres by 3,4 metres, has been featured in numerous TV dramas. The LED lights in the central part of the 'eye' slowly rotate.

490 IKEFUKURO STATUE

Outside Ikebukuro Station (JR, Tokyo Metro, Seibu Ikebukuro Line, Tobu Tojo Line)
Toshima-ku ⑪

Fukuro means 'owl' in Japanese but also sounds like *fu* (which is a prefix meaning 'no') and *kuro* (trouble). So *fukuro* is considered as a symbol of being free of trouble, without a hassle. *Fukuro* also rhymes with Ikebukuro. Ikefukuro is located near Kita-kaisatsu (the north ticket barrier).

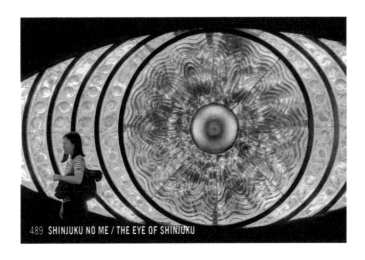

489 SHINJUKU NO ME / THE EYE OF SHINJUKU

5 things you should know before
GETTING ON A TRAIN

---

491 DIFFERENT TICKETS FOR DIFFERENT TRAIN OPERATORS

There are several train operators on Tokyo's transport system: two subway operators, JR, and a few private railway companies. You must buy a ticket for each operator unless you have a special ticket for travelling on the trains of two connected operators. Consider buying a prepaid card, such as Suica or Pasmo.

492 PAY AT YOUR DESTINATION

Unlike many other countries, Japan allows people to adjust their fare at their destination. This means that you have a chance to pay the correct price at the end of the journey, even if you mistakenly bought a cheaper ticket. There are no plain-clothes ticket inspectors on board.

493 NO TALKING ON YOUR MOBILE PHONE ON THE TRAIN

Tokyo's train operators do NOT allow passengers to talk on the phone while on the train even though they have excellent reception. People just keep quiet and text. Do not forget to turn off the sound of your device either.

494 **ESCALATOR ETIQUETTE – STAND LEFT**

Nobody knows who decided this, but people stand left on the escalator in Tokyo (they do the opposite in Osaka by the way.) But do not walk or run on the right even if your train has arrived at the platform. Tokyo operates a frequent train service.

495 **LINE UP ACCORDING TO THE MARKS ON THE PLATFORM**

When you look at a platform, there are marks that tell you where the doors are. In other words, they tell you where you can get on the train. Usually, these marks make passengers queue in two lines. Sometimes, they also indicate the area where you can wait for the next train.

495 LINE UP ACCORDING TO THE MARKS ON THE PLATFORM

5 facts about
JAPANESE TOILETS

---

496 JAPANESE-STYLE TOILET

Japan has 'squat' toilets although they are few and far between nowadays as Western-style toilets are adopted more frequently in the home. Used toilet paper should always be flushed down the toilet – whether Japanese or Western.

497 RELATIVELY CLEAN

Even the public toilets in subway stations, in parks, or on the streets, are relatively clean. However, if you are a clean freak, carrying hand sanitiser with you is recommended as some of the public toilets do not have soap.

498 WASHLET

Washlet is a product invented by the Japanese company TOTO. If you press a button, a nozzle appears and washes your buttocks with lukewarm water. Please do not press the button when you are not sitting on the toilet.

499 OTOHIME

Japanese women do not like being heard when they use the toilet, so toilets have a machine that produces a flushing sound. If you don't mind this then don't bother using it. Be careful not to press an Otohime button in error when you want to flush.

500 HOW TO FLUSH

There are plenty of different types. Push down handles, pull up handles, press buttons, sensors, automatic flushing toilets… It is complicated, even for Japanese people, so it must be even more difficult when you don't read Japanese. Look for a clue. Good luck.

INDEX

COLOPHON

EDITING *and* COMPOSING — Yukiko Tajima

GRAPHIC DESIGN — Joke Gossé and Tinne Luyten

PHOTOGRAPHY — Koji Ishikawa — www.koji-ishikawa.com

COVER IMAGE — Nezu Art Museum (secret 346)

The addresses in this book have been selected after thorough independent
research by the author, in collaboration with Luster Publishers. The selection
is solely based on personal evaluation of the business by the author. Nothing
in this book was published in exchange for payment or benefits of any kind.

D/2018/12.005/4
ISBN 978 94 6058 2202
NUR 510, 517

© 2018, Luster, Antwerp
First edition, March 2018 — First reprint, September 2018
www.lusterweb.com — www.the500hiddensecrets.com
info@lusterweb.com

Printed in Italy by Printer Trento.

MIX
Paper from
responsible sources
FSC® C015829
www.fsc.org